CHINESE CASH

BY

O. D. CRESSWELL

Published by

Sanford J. Durst
Numismatic Publications
New York, New York
and
Spink & Sons Ltd.
St. James
London, England

BY APPOINTMENT
TO HER MAJESTY THE QUEEN
MEDALLISTS

BY APPOINTMENT
TO H.R.H. THE DUKE OF EDINBURGH
MEDALLISTS.

Sanford J. Durst
133 East 58th Street
New York, NY 10022

and

Spink & Sons Ltd.
5-7 King Street
St. James
London, England

Printed in the United States of America

INTRODUCTION

The long series of Chinese Cash, extending for more than two thousand years, has many attractions for the coin collector. Many of the rulers who have shaped the history of one of the world's great civilisations, Emperor and Rebel alike, issued coins with easily identifiable legends. The coins were cast from the base metals copper and iron and countless varieties are to be found. Many of the coins in this series may be obtained at modest prices and the condition of the coin, as long as the legend is clearly legible, is relatively unimportant. From the mint names, first used regularly by the T'ang Emperors, we can trace the expansion of China while the diminished sizes of the coins mark out the periods when inflation, that far from modern economic ailment, affected the country. Above all the Chinese Cash series is one where no knowledge of the language is necessary. In the present book will be found all the legends used on Chinese Cash together with illustrations so arranged that identification of any coin becomes a simple matter.

The illustrations are not intended as examples of Chinese calligraphy but show the appearance of each coin. Each drawing, where possible, has been made from the actual coin and when these were unobtainable Eugene Y.C. Wang has earned my sincere gratitude by providing copies of rubbings taken from coins in the National Museum of History in Taipei. In one case where no coin of the type was known to exist Taipei Museum were able to provide a rubbing of a mould and from this the illustration was made. In only four cases were illustrations impossible to provide as no specimen of the coin could be traced. It must be stressed that there are wide variations in the diameter of coins of any issue - I have noted a difference of ten mms between the largest and smallest examples in some cases - and this must be remembered when using the illustrations. Where varying sizes differentiate issues of coins with the same obverse legend these have been noted in the text and for the Pan Liang and Wu Chu series a summary will be found in the Appendix A.

I have resisted the temptation to make facile estimates of rarity as it has been my experience that one collector may have several specimens of a coin which to another has remained unobtainable. Some coins will be rare because of the short period during which they were cast and others because they were issued in small quantities to meet the restricted commercial needs of a small population under a rebel leader or the Emperor of an Irregular Dynasty. Again the widespread use of paper money in Yüan China meant that the issues of coins would be on a small scale while the Ming Supplementary issues were cast in token quantities only. It must also be remembered that all through China's history as the price of copper rose, coins, and inevitably the older coins in circulation, would be melted down for their metal value and conversely when the price of metal fell discarded metal objects would be melted down to provide a new coinage. However, the Regular Dynasties, at least, did issue cash by the thousand million and sufficient have survived to make them less rare than their age would lead us to suppose.

The text has been divided into three sections, Regular Dynasties, Irregular Dynasties and the coins of Pretenders and Rebels. The first and last sections are self explanatory and the Irregular Dynasties are best described as lines of Emperors who ruled over regions, usually small, on the borders of China and while their coinage was Chinese in type they themselves played a small part in Chinese history. The distinction between an Irregular Dynasty and a Rebel Leader is a fine one but perhaps the best way is to express the difference is that of time, as a Rebel Leader rarely lasted long enough to establish a dynasty.

With the translation of the legends I have been very fortunate to have received the willing assistance of Mrs. Marion Cayton of Bristol, formerly a missionary in Manchuria, but where errors have occurred I must accept sole responsibility. The phrases YÜAN PAO and T'UNG PAO have been translated throughout the text as ' Coinage '. The character YÜAN can signify ' First ' and while there is some evidence for its use on the initial coinage of an issue it is not conclusive enough to justify translating YÜAN PAO as ' Initial Coinage ' in every case. Normally the legend of a coin is read Top, Bottom, Right and Left, or from Right to Left on a coin with a two character legend, and any exceptions to this have been noted in the appropriate section of the text.

In every case where it was possible I have used the Temple Title to describe the Emperor. An Emperor would have five names - (a) a family name, (b) a personal name which follows the family name as Chinese reads from right to left, (c) a Posthumous Temple Title, (d) a Posthumous Memorial Title which could contain many characters and (e) a Title given to his reign and by association to himself, which could and often was altered more than once during his lifetime. The reign titles have been denoted as Periods throughout the text. An example will make the matter clearer. The first ruler of the Ming Dynasty was Yüan-chang of the family of Chu, therefore his full name was Chu Yüan-chang. His reign had the title of Hung Wu and so during his lifetime he would be known as the Hung Wu Emperor. After his death he was given the Temple Title of T'ai Tsu and a Memorial Title of more than twenty characters. The Temple Title has therefore the advantages of brevity and simplicity.

I should like to take this opportunity to pay a tribute to the late Major Protassowicki, a student of Oriental numismatics of great learning and even greater charm. His learning was made freely available to any collector beginning the study of Chinese coins and it is in the hope that this work will take the place of a guide such as he was that the following pages have been penned.

Belfast 1970

O.D. Cresswell

DYNASTIES OF THE REGULAR LINE

Ch'in Dynasty 255 B.C. - 207 B.C.
Western Han Dynasty 206 B.C. - 24 A.D.
Interregnum Wang Mang 6 A.D. - 23 A.D.
Eastern Han Dynasty 25 A.D. - 221 A.D.
Epoch of the Three Kingdoms 221 A.D. - 280 A.D.
Minor Han Dynasty 221 A.D. . - 265 A.D.
Wu Dynasty 222 A.D. - 280 A.D.
Ch'in Dynasty 256 A.D. - 420 A.D.
Epoch of Division between North and South 420 A.D. - 581 A.D.
Liu Sung Dynasty 420 A.D. - 479 A.D.
Liang Dynasty 502 A.D. - 557 A.D.
Ch'ên Dynasty 557 A.D. - 589 A.D.
Northern Wei Dynasty 386 A.D. - 534 A.D.
Northern Ch'i Dynasty 550 A.D. - 577 A.D.
Northern Chou Dynasty 557 A.D. - 581 A.D.
Sui Dynasty 581 A.D. - 618 A.D.
T'ang Dynasty 618 A.D. - 907 A.D.
Epoch of the Five Dynasties 907 A.D. - 960 A.D.
Later Liang Dynasty 907 A.D. - 922 A.D.
Later T'ang Dynasty 923 A.D. - 935 A.D.
Later Chin Dynasty 936 A.D. - 947 A.D.
Later Han Dynasty 947 A.D. - 951 A.D.
Later Chou Dynasty 951 A.D. - 960 A.D.
Sung Dynasties (North and South) 960 A.D. - 1279 A.D.
Yüan Dynasty 1279 A.D. - 1367 A.D.
Ming Dynasty 1368 A.D. - 1644 A.D.
Ch'ing Dynasty 1616 A.D. - 1911 A.D.

THE CH'IN DYNASTY 255-207 B.C.

The year 221 B.C. is an important date in Chinese history as in that year, after a fifty year struggle had subdued the Chou and other states, the Ch'in Dynasty brought the peoples of North and Central China under one ruler and in that year Chêng Wang assumed the title of Emperor. Two years later his successor Shih Huang Ti symbolised his position as Emperor by making an ascent of the sacred mountain Tai to perform sacrifice for the Chinese people. In 213 B.C. Li Ssu, the Prime Minister, ordered the destruction of all written histories of the earlier dynasties and so coins cast before the Ch'in Dynasty can only be dated approximately by the use of archaeological data. Those who attempted to conceal copies of the earlier histories were condemned to slave labour on the Great Wall of China, over a thousand miles of which were commenced by Shih Huang Ti. Not only did this dynasty give to China its name but also the present structure of its written language, a further unifying factor whose importance can hardly be overstressed.

In 221 B.C. Shih Huang Ti became Emperor and one of his first tasks was to provide a common currency for the newly formed Chinese Empire. He ordered the casting of coins weighing twelve Chu and bearing the legend PAN LIANG. When first issued these coins had a weight of approximately ten grams and a diameter of forty mms. As the minting of coins was not a state monopoly casting by private individuals soon reduced the weight to six grams and the diameter to twenty eight mms. Most of these coins have an inner rim but some of the ' private ' issues have the legend reading from left to right and lack the inner rim.

Shih Huang Ti died after a reign of eleven years and the two succeeding rulers of this dynasty, his son Êrh Shih and grandson Ch'in Wang, ruled a mere four years between them.

Emperor SHIH HUANG TI. 221-210 B.C.

No.1. Legend. PAN LIANG (One half ounce).
(Note. This issue of Pan Liang coins has an inner rim.)

THE WESTERN HAN DYNASTY 206 B.C.-24 A.D.

While the Ch'in Dynasty brought the benefits of unity to China it was by nature oppressive and popular opposition to it was led by Liu Pang, a peasant, and Hsiang Yu, a General of the earlier Chou Dynasty. When Ch'in Wang, the last emperor of the Ch'in Dynasty was deposed the two leaders divided China between them, Liu Pang taking as his kingdom an area in Shen - Hsi and Ssu - Ch'uan called Han after a local river. Shortly after Liu Pang defeated his one time ally Hsiang Yu and established the Han Dynasty over all China, establishing his capital in Chang An. At this time the population of Han China was in the region of sixty million, roughly equal to that of the Roman Empire in Europe at its greatest extent. Four years after seizing control Liu Pang took the title of Emperor with the name Kao Ti.

Preoccupied with the task of establishing his authority the Emperor Kao Ti left the casting of coins to private enterprise and the natural outcome of this policy was a rapid deterioration of the coinage. While still bearing the legend PAN LIANG the weight of a cash fell as low as a quarter of a gram and the diameter varied from ten to twenty mms. The common people derisively called them " Yü Kieh ", Elm Leaves from their light weight.

Emperor KAO TI 206 - 195 B.C.

No. 2. Legend. Pan Liang. (One half ounce).

(Note. Easily distinguished from No.1 by its diameter of ten to twenty mms.)

On the death of Kao Ti his son Hsiao Hui succeeded to the throne and during his reign of seven years the Elm Leaves continued to be produced. On the death of Hsiao Hui his mother Kao Hou made his infant son, the child of a concubine, emperor but he was never enthroned nor was a title granted to him. The unfortunate child was imprisoned and put to death in 184 B.C. and Kao Hou, who had acted as Regent, took the throne as Empress of China. In an attempt to stabilise the coinage the Empress Kao Hou established the Pan Liang at a weight of eight Chu. The coin still bore the legend Pan Liang, one half ounce, although the ounce being divisible into twenty four Chu it in reality weighed a third of an ounce. The initial issue of these coins weighed about six grams with a diameter of thirty two mms but since private casting was permitted the weight soon fell to four grams with a diameter of twenty five mms.

EMPRESS KAO HOU 187 - 180 B.C.

No.3. Legend. PAN LIANG (One half ounce).

(Note. This issue of Pan Liang coins is distinguishable by its diameter varying between twenty five and thirty two mms.)

When the Empress Kao Hou died in 180 B.C. she was succeeded by her son Wên Ti who ruled for twenty two years. In his reign yet another attempt at stability was made. The weight of the PAN LIANG coin was fixed at four Chu, one sixth of an ounce, while the legend PAN LIANG, one half of an ounce remained unaltered. The initial weight of four grams soon fell to three grams, roughly the weight of a copper cash over the centuries, while the diameter varies from twenty seven to twenty four mms.

EMPEROR WÊN TI 179 - 157 B.C.

No. 4. Legend. PAN LIANG (One half ounce).

(Note. Diameter from twenty seven to twenty four mms. Weight that of usual cash.)

Hsiao Ching succeeded his father Wên Ti on the throne in 157 B.C. and reigned for sixteen years. During his reign there were no innovations in the coinage so the Pan Liang of four Chu continued to be cast. So with a mintage period of some forty years and its approximation to the normal one cash in weight this coin survived in greater numbers than the other Pan Liang issues and is probably the most commonly met with today.

In 140 B.C. Wu Ti, the son of Hsiao Ching became Emperor. He is perhaps the most significant of all the Han Emperors and his long reign of fifty three years saw important changes in the coinage of China. He earned the title of Wu Ti the Brave from his campaigns to subdue the nomadic tribesmen who raided into North and West China and after many successful campaigns brought Mongolia, South Manchuria and large parts of Korea and Turkistan under Chinese rule. This freeing of the overland routes to India from raiders greatly increased trade between China and the Greek States of India. From India the silks and porcelain of China spread to Roman Europe and in return the caravans carried wine and glass to the court of Wu Ti.

In a last attempt to stabilise the Pan Liang coinage the weight was decreed to be three Chu, the legend remaining unchanged though the coin now weighed one eighth of an ounce instead of the stated half ounce. There are two varieties of this coin. Firstly a Pan Liang with a diameter of twenty five mms and a weight of about two grams. This Pan Liang is readily distinguished by its having the rim on the obverse turned up. The second variety, an extremely rare coin has the Chinese numeral SAN, three, below the aperture. This is the only Chinese coin bearing a legend with three characters. Iron examples of the first variety are to be found, probably unofficial issues.

In 140 B.C. an attempt was made to issue a coin with the legend SAN CHU (Three Chu) but the common people demanded the Pan Liang coins they were used to and the attempt was a failure, being withdrawn three years later. But in 118 B.C. the Emperor Wu Ti decided that the time had come to do away with the Pan Liang coinage and issued coins weighing five Chu and bearing the legend WU CHU (Five Chu). The issue was immediately successful and can perhaps be described as the most acceptable coinage ever issued by any state in the world as for over seven centuries without any change in the legend it was issued by nine dynasties of the Regular Line and some twenty three Irregular Dynasties. There are untold varieties and Chinese students of numismatics claim, on the evidence of coin moulds, to be able to allocate these many varieties to their correct dates of issue. Most of the varieties offer differences too minute for practical purposes but those which are readily discernible are listed under their appropriate dynasty and emperor. It is often overlooked that the discovery of a dated coin mould showing a certain variation cannot be taken to mean that all coins of that date show a similar variation and indeed it must be remembered that a similar variation may have been issued by a ruler of another dynasty in a different century. Where WU CHU coins show none of the varieties listed the only method of dating depends on the style of lettering as this does show change over the centuries. If the right hand component of the character CHU is examined some coins will show a square outline while others will have a rounded outline. Those with the square outline are the older and may be dated between 100 B.C. and 200 A.D. and those with the rounded shape between 200 A.D. and 600 A.D. Indeed without being considered too inaccurate the first type may be ascribed to the Western and Eastern Han dynasties and the second type to the dynasties which followed them. I know of no distinguishing variety which can be assigned to the original issue of Wu Chus made by the Emperor Wu Ti and the coin illustrated as No. 8 is a typical Wu Chu of the Han Dynasties.

EMPEROR WU TI 140 B.C. - 87 B.C.

No. 5. Legend. PAN LIANG (One half ounce).
(Note. This issue has the outer obverse edge turned up to form a rudimentary rim.)

No. 6. Legend. PAN LIANG SAN. (One half ounce, three).
(Note. The only Chinese coin with a legend of three characters.)

No. 7. Legend. SAN CHU (Three Chus)

No. 8. Legend. WU CHU (Five Chus)
(Note. This coin is a typical Wu Chu coin of the Han Dynasties as there is no variation known on the issue made by this emperor.)

On the death of the Emperor WU TI the throne passed to a brother Hsiao Chao but it is not possible to assign any Wu Chu coins to his reign. His successor on the throne was Hsiao Hsüan Ti, a great grandson of the Emperor Wu Ti. He ruled China from 74 B.C. to 48

B.C. and to his reign is assigned the issue of Wu Chu coins with a raised rim above the aperture on the obverse. A coin mould has been found with this distinguishing feature and bearing the date 60 B.C.

EMPEROR HSIAO HSÜAN TI 74 B.C. - 48 B.C.

No.9. Legend. WU CHU (Five Chus)

(Note. This issue has a raised rim above the obverse aperture.)

Before describing the coinage of the usurper Wang Mang, who brought the Western Han Dynasty to a close it is necessary to include here a class of 'coins' which on the surface purport to belong to the Han era. It is the custom at certain festivals in China to present to children a specimen of the old Cash coins, a custom still continued in Taiwan to this day. With the natural disappearance of the older coins commercial interests produced copies or rather fancied copies for sale for this purpose. These copies are usually described as amulets and are to be found in the section of catalogues devoted to that type of piece. As inexperienced collectors may be misled into thinking they have discovered an old coin so far undescribed I have thought it best to include here two specimens typical of two entirely different types of these pieces.

No.10. Legend. WU CHU (Five Chus)

This piece is so much larger than a normal Wu Chu coin that had it been current at the same time it would have certainly been melted down and turned into several coins. The left hand component of the character CHU is a mere caricature of the style of writing used in the Han Dynasty.

No.11. Legend. WU CHU SHIH CHIEN. (Thousands of Wu Chu Coins).

There are many varieties of this second type of 'coin' with stated values ranging from ten thousand to ten million cash. It is inconceivable that a copper coin could have been current with such a value when its intrinsic value would only be a dozen or so Wu Chu and had it been, the temptation to melt down a few of the normal Wu Chu coins and cast a copy would have been irresistable. It is difficult to equate currencies so widely spaced in time as the Wu Chu and our own but since a junior army officer in Han times received some three hundred cash a month the purchasing power of a Wu Chu coin must have been about two shillings. To imagine an economy working on the basis of a two shilling coin with the next highest value some five thousand pounds is not possible. Many of these 'coins' bear on the reverse a date given in the form of the year period of one of the Han emperors and at this time these dates did not appear on the coinage nor were they to do so for many centuries. These considerations show that these pieces cannot date from Han times and they probably are the products of small foundries in the late nineteenth centuries. They are however a fascinating series and well worth inclusion in a collection. Besides their interest as copies of 'coins' they are impressive in their size and are invariably well cast. They range in size up to about one hundred and forty mms.

THE INTERREGNUM OF WANG MANG 6 A.D. - 23 A.D.

When the Emperor Hsiao Ai died in the year 1 A.D. Wang Mang, a nephew of the Dowager Empress Yüan Ti, served his successor Hsiao Ping Ti as Prime Minister. Since the newly enthroned Emperor was only eight years old Wang Mang was in a position of almost absolute power and rather than lose this position when Hsiao Ping Ti assumed personal control he had the Emperor poisoned in the year 6 A.D. His successor on the throne was named Ying, a great-great-grandson of the Emperor Hsiao Hsuan Ti (See No. 9) aged two years. Wang Mang 'served' him as Regent for three years and then deposed him and took the title of Emperor for himself. During his years as Regent large numbers of the Spade, Pu and Knife coins of the Chou Dynasty, 1122 - 255 B.C., had been unearthed and had aroused considerable interest. Wang Mang claimed descent from the legendary Emperor Yü Ti Shun, the earliest recorded ruler of China, and wished to use coinage such as he imagined was in use in the China of his ancestor. He issued Knife and Pu coins but since these are not 'cash' I have not included them in the text, although illustrations will be found labelled A and B on the seoond plate of coins. Omitting the Knife and Pu coins Wang Mang issued no fewer than seven types of cash coins in his capacity as Regent and three more as Emperor.

Despite his merits from the point of view of the coin collector Wang Mang was a tyrannical ruler and opposition to his rule grew, culminating in the revolt of his troops in 23 A.D. when he was beheaded and the Han Dynasty reinstated. However as the capital was established in Lo-yang the continuation of the Han Dynasty is regarded as a new Dynasty and called the Eastern Han Dynasty.

WANG MANG as REGENT 6 A.D. - 9 A.D.

No.12. Legend. TA CH'ÜAN WU SHIH (Large coin fifty cash)
No.13. Legend. CHUANG CH'ÜAN SSU SHIH (Robust coin forty cash)
No.14. Legend. CHUNG CH'ÜAN SAN SHIH (Middle coin thirty cash)
No.15. Legend. YU CH'ÜAN ÊRH SHIH (Young coin twenty cash)
No.16. Legend. YAO CH'ÜAN YI SHIH (Tender coin ten cash)
No.17. Legend. HSIAO CH'ÜAN CHIH YI (Small coin one cash)

The legends of all these coins are written in seal script and the size of the coins varies considerably so the illustrations are to be taken only as a guide to the inscriptions. It would seem that only the TA CH'ÜAN coins were issued in any quantity as the others are rare pieces, the HSIAO CH'ÜAN coins being the rarest of them all.

(Note. See under the rebel Kung Sun Shih, No. 22, for examples of such coins with corrupt legends.)

No.18. Legend. CH'I TAO (A graving knife)

This coin, whose legend is in seal script, was authorised in the year 7 A.D. but it is doubtful if it was issued in any quantity. Some examples are to be found inlaid in gold, a practice also to be found in some examples of the Knife and Pu coinage issued by Wang Mang.

WANG MANG as EMPEROR 9 A.D. - 23 A.D.

No.19. Legend. HUO CH'ÜAN (Coin for exchange)

The legend is written in seal script.

No.20. Legend. PU CH'ÜAN (Current coin)

These coins are to be found both with and without an inner rim. At first glance it would seem that the rimless coins are not official issues but this is not necessarily so as those with an inner rim show a greater variation in diameter than those lacking a rim. (17 - 23 mms compared with 21 - 22 mms.) The style of writing is known as the 'suspended needle'. It must be carefully noted that the central stroke of the character CH'ÜAN is broken as this helps to distinguish this issue of Pu Ch'üans from that of the Northern Chou Dynasty where the central stroke is unbroken. See No. 56.

No.21. Legend. TA CH'ÜAN SHIH WU (Large coin fifteen cash)

The legend of this rare coin is written in seal script. In the year 14 A.D. Wang Mang issued Pu coins valued at twenty five Huo Ch'üans and devalued the Ta Ch'uan coins (No.12) from fifty cash to fifteen cash. This coin must have been cast in that year.

In the troubled times following the death of Wang Mang a rebel leader Kung Sun Shih set himself up in Ssu-Ch'uan Province and issued coins. To him are attributed copies of the coins of Wang Mang, Nos. 12 - 16, which have errors in the characters in the legends. He is also said to have issued iron coins with the legend HUO CH'ÜAN and iron Wu Chus. These latter lack the distinguishing features of the iron Wu Chus of the Emperor Wu Ti of the Liang Dynasty in 523 A.D. (See No. 46.) Probably many of the iron coins attributed to this rebel leader and most of the coppers with errors in their legends were in reality issued by 'private' coiners but as they belong to this period I have thought it better to gather them together under one heading.

REBEL LEADER KUNG SUN SHIH 24 A.D. - 36 A.D.

No.22. Legend. WU CHU (Five Chus)

Notes. (a) The coin is made of iron

(b) The cross strokes of the character CHU are straight.

THE EASTERN HAN DYNASTY 25 A.D. - 221 A.D.

When the Usurper Wang Mang was killed the Han Dynasty was re-established by the Emperor Kuang Wu Ti with its capital at Lo-yang, hence the Dynastic name of Eastern Han. Kuang Wu Ti claimed to be a ninth generation descendant of the Emperor Kao Tsu who had founded the Western Han Dynasty and is known in Chinese history as " The Bright and Brave ". A better claim to fame is perhaps his establishing the first Chinese university in his capital city. In the year 40 A.D. the coinage of the Usurper Wang Mang was withdrawn from circulation and replaced by a re-issue of the Wu Chu coinage. A mould dated the eighteenth year of this reign bears the distinguishing feature of no inner rim on the obverse and Wu Chu coins of this type are assigned to this reign.

EMPEROR KUANG WU TI 25 A.D. - 57 A.D.

No.23. Legend. WU CHU (Five Chus)

(Note. This issue lacks an inner obverse rim.)

Ten other emperors of this dynasty followed Kuang Wu Ti on the throne of China, all issuing Wu Chu coins, unfortunately indistinguishable, but a mould dated the eighteenth year of the Emperor Ling Ti enables us to assign some of the Wu Chus to his reign. These coins lack the inner obverse rim and have short diagonal dashes running out from the corners of the obverse or reverse aperture. Ling Ti was a sixth generation descendant of Kuang Wu Ti, the founder of the Eastern Han Dynasty.

EMPEROR LING TI 168 A.D. - 188 A.D.

No.24. Legend. WU CHU (Five Chus)

(Note. This issue lacks the inner rim on the obverse and shows short diagonal dashes on either obverse or reverse.)

THE EPOCH OF THE THREE KINGDOMS. 221 A.D. - 280 A.D.

On the death of the last Emperor of the Eastern Han Dynasty, Hsien Ti in 221 A.D. China was divided into three Kingdoms, The Minor Han, The Wei and The Wu. As no coins are to be assigned to the Wei Dynasty we can ignore them and concentrate on the other two dynasties.

THE MINOR HAN DYNASTY 221 A.D. - 265 A.D.

When the Eastern Han Dynasty collapsed in 221 A.D. General Chao Lieh Ti, stationed in Ssu-Ch'uan Province established the Minor Han Dynasty. His realm was a secure enclave in the mountains, open to attack only from Tibet and along the Yangtse valley. In this latter region continuous fighting went on with the armies of the Wei Dynasty successfully at first under the leadership of the Emperor and on his death of the Prime Minister Chu Ko Liang. On the death of the latter in 234 A.D. the fortunes of the Dynasty declined and it was eventually absorbed by the Wei Dynasty.

During this dynasty trade declined and only the need to recompense his troops on the capture of the city of Cheng Tu led the Emperor Chao Lieh Ti to make an issue of coins. Some of these coins bear on the reverse the mint name of Chien Wei in Ssu-Ch'uan, the town of issue, the first time a mint name had appeared on Chinese coins. Others bear either of the numerals one or two to indicate their year of issue. Some of these coins were cast in iron, the first official use of this metal for coinage. The brevity of the legend on the second type of this reign is a clear indication of the haste with which the Emperor had this issue produced as also is the production of coins where the legend reads from left to right instead of the normal right to left.

EMPEROR CHAO LIEH TI 221 A.D. - 223 A.D.

No.25. Legend. CHIH PAI WU CHU (One hundred Wu Chus)
No.26. Legend. CHIH PAI (One hundred)

THE WU DYNASTY 222 A.D. - 280 A.D.

The Wu Dynasty was established in 222 A.D. by the Emperor Ta Ti in south eastern China with Nanking as its capital city, assuming the title of Emperor seven years later. The region was inhabited mainly by Tai people whose economy was based on rice growing in the fertile valleys. The Wu Dynasty fought many campaigns against the armies of the Wei Dynasty but their most effective weapon was intriguing with the Manchurian tribes who threatened the northern frontier of their enemies and by a judicious mixture of force and intrigue they maintained their independence until they were subdued by the armies of the Western Ch'in Dynasty which briefly reunited China at the end of the Epoch of the Three Kingdoms.

EMPEROR TA TI 229 A.D. - 252 A.D.

No.27. Legend. TA CH'ÜAN WU PAI (Large coin five hundred cash)
No.28. Legend. TA CH'ÜAN TANG CH'IEN (Large coin one thousand cash)
No.29. Legend. TA CH'ÜAN ÊRH CH'IEN (Large coin two thousand cash)

The legends of all three coins are written in seal script and are to be read in a clockwise direction. The first coin was issued in 236 A. D. followed by the others two years later and the rapidly increasing denominations are a clear indication of the shortage of copper in this regionof China coupled with ever increasing inflation.

On the death of Ta Ti in 252 A.D. he was succeeded by his younger son Fei Ti who was deposed by his brother Ching Ti six years later. His coins bear a four character legend where two of the characters give the year period, a method of dating here appearing for the first time on a Chinese coin but destined to be the normal type of coinage for more than a thousand years.

EMPEROR FEI TI 252 A.D. - 258 A.D.
PERIOD. T'AI P'ING 256 A.D. - 258 A.D.

No.30. Legend. T'AI P'ING PAI CHIEN (One hundred cash of Great Peace)

No.31. Legend. T'AI P'ING CHIN PAI (One hundred cash of Great Peace)

The Emperor Ching Ti ruled for six years and was succeeded by a nephew who is variously referred to as Mo Ti, Kuei Ming Hou or Wu Ch'êng Ti. This ruler was deposed in the year 280 A.D. when the dynasty and with it the Epoch of the Three Kingdoms came to an end. During the closing years of this dynasty was produced a coin, described as No. 32, but it is not known whether or not it is an official issue or produced by some governor or war lord.

INDETERMINATE RULER Circa 265 A.D.

No.32. Legend. TING P'ING YI PAI. (One hundred cash of Settled Peace)

Judging from the history of this period the choice of the legend, Settled Peace, must have been more a prayer for the future than a reflection of contemporary conditions in this portion of China.

THE CH'IN DYNASTIES 256 A.D. - 420 A.D.

These two dynasties reunited China for a short period between the Epoch of the Three Kingdoms and the Division between the North and the South. The Western Ch'in Dynasty was founded by Wu Ti in 256 A.D., though he did not assume the title of Emperor for another ten years, with Lo-yang as his capital city. In the closing years of the Dynasty Ch'ang An became the capital. Wu Ti won the leadership of the Dynasty by the intrigues of a widely spread family and in these intrigues lay the seeds of the dissolution of the Dynasty sixty years later. The Emperor Wu Ti was faced by two problems, large standing armies at a time when there seemed to be no obvious external threat and a grave shortage of metal for coinage. Attempting to solve both problems at once he ordered the disbandment of the armies and the handing in of their weapons to provide the necessary metal for a recoinage. This proved a failure as the troops dispersed, retaining their weapons, and indeed many of them migrated to the Hsiung-nu and Hsien-pi tribes north of China and exchanged their weapons for land, thus preparing these tribes for their later incursions into China. The only coins to be assigned to this Dynasty are very small Wu Chus with incomplete legends, clear indications of the straits to which the Emperor Wu Ti was put to provide the recoinage so desperately needed by China.

EMPEROR WU TI 266 A.D. - 290 A.D.

No.33. Legend. WU CHU (Five Chus)
(Note. This issue of Wu Chu coins is to be distinguished by (a) a diameter of fifteen or sixteen mms and (b) incomplete legends.)

In the year 317 A.D. Ching Tsung established the Eastern Ch'in Dynasty with its capital at Chien Kang. This dynasty, weak and ineffective, was composed of Tibetan tribesmen in the province of Shen-Hsi with a ruling class of a mixture of Chinese and Hun families. The only coinage attributable to this dynasty belongs to the Emperor Hsiao Wu Ti, a grandson of the founder of the dynasty, no fewer than seven other rulers having held the throne in the fifty years since the death of Chung Tsung in 323 A.D. This dynasty was also faced with a drain of metal from China to the tribesmen to the north and the export of all metals was forbidden. It is a charming thought that these Tartar people claimed that they need the metal to fashion trumpets and drums. Hsiao Wu Ti was followed on the throne of China by two sons who ruled until the Empire of China was divided into the North and the South in 420 A.D.

THE EMPEROR HSIAO WU TI 372 A.D. - 396 A.D.
PERIOD T'AI YUAN 376 A.D. - 396 A.D.

No.34. Legend. T'AI YUAN HO CHUAN (Source of exchange of Great Beginning)

(Note. This is the second Chinese coin to use the year period in its legend.)

EPOCH OF THE DIVISION BETWEEN THE NORTH AND THE SOUTH

Between the years 420 A.D. and 581 A.D. China broke up into a bewildering array of states, constantly at war with each other and absorbing each other. No fewer than nine dynasties ruled portions of China during this period and six of these dynasties, Sung, Liang, Ch'ên, Northern Wei, Northern Ch'i and Northern Chou issued coins. These six dynasties will be considered separately.

LIU SUNG DYNASTY 420 A.D. - 479 A.D.

To distinguish this dynasty from the greater Sung dynasty of the tenth century it is called the Liu Sung after its founder Liu Yü, a general who gained many successes in Shen-Hsi province in 415 A.D., thus becoming the power behind the throne and as usual in Chinese history deposed the puppet emperor and assumed the imperial power in name as well as in fact. This dynasty fought long and usually unsuccessful wars against the Toba and after sustaining a disastrous defeat on the banks of the Yangtse in 450 A.D. were forced to pay an annual tribute to them. Eight emperors ruled this dynasty, each one more ineffective than his predecessor and in 479 A.D. they were absorbed by the Southern Ch'i Dynasty founded by Hsiao Tao Ch'êng.

THE EMPEROR WÊN TI 424 A.D. - 453 A.D.

No.35. Legend. SSU CHU (Four Chus)
These coins were issued in 430 A.D. by the Emperor Wên Ti, the third ruler of this dynasty and a son of the founder Liu Yu who had taken the title of Kao Tsu on taking the throne.

No.36. Legend. WU CHU (Five Chus)
These are the largest of the Wu Chu coins and readily distinguishable by their prominent rim. They weighed eight Chus and were to circulate at a rate of One Wu Chu equalling two Ssu Chu coins, a proceeding which must have led to confusion to say the least.

THE EMPEROR HSIAO WU TI 454 A.D. - 464 A.D.

No.37. Legend. HSIAO CHIEN (A son's duty performed)

These coins were issued in 454 A.D. and the legend refers to the funeral rites of his father the Emperor Wên Ti. The reverse bears the value SSU CHU (Four Chus)

On the death of Hsiao Wu Ti in 464 A.D. he was succeeded by his eldest son Ch'ien Fei Ti who also marked his father's funerary rites by making an issue of Hsiao Chien coins, easily distinguishable from the earlier issue by their lighter weight and by the absence of the value on the reverse. Ch'ien Fei Ti ruled a bare two years and yet issued two other types of coin, both naturally rare pieces.

THE EMPEROR CH'IEN FEI TI 464 A.D. - 466 A.D.

No.38. Legend. HSIAO CHIEN (A son's duty performed)
(Note. Lack of reverse value and lighter weight.)

PERIOD. CHING HO 465 A.D.

No.39. Legend. CHING HO (Brilliant Concord)
No.40. Legend. YUNG KUANG (Unceasing Light)

When Ch'ien Fei Ti died in 466 A.D. an uncle Ming Ti became Emperor and issued yet another Hsiao Chien coin, even lighter than that of his predecessor and like the earlier issue lacking a reverse value. It is difficult to distinguish the coins of the Emperor Ming Ti from Ch'ien Fei Ti as at this time counterfeiting the imperial coinage was something of a national sport in China. The penalty of losing a hand was apparently no deterrent and from time to time the more skilful of the counterfeiters were hired as workmen in the imperial mints. Making a mould in clay, using a genuine coin, would be a simple task and the whole operation of casting copies could be carried on as a home craft to pass the winter evenings. All through the history of China the use of copper coins possessing their intrinsic value as metal led to coins being melted down for metal as money lost its value through inflation and the opposite process of melting down weapons and implements to cast coins when the value of money passed the metal content of the coin. This dual process has led to the rarity of so many of the earlier Chinese coins as even though they were cast by the million they were melted down in similar numbers and in the case of small issues where only a few thousand were cast it is hardly surprising that some today cannot be found at all.

THE EMPEROR MING TI 466 A.D. - 472 A.D.

No.41. Legend. HSIAO CHIEN (A son's duty performed)
(Note. Smaller, diameter about twenty mms, than No. 38.)

THE LIANG DYNASTY 502 A.D. - 557 A.D.

This dynasty ruled those parts of Southern China which were free from Tartar rule and replaced the Ch'i Dynasty which in its turn had succeeded the Liu Sung Dynasty. The dynasty was founded by Wu Ti who took the title of Kao Tsu on assuming the imperial title. He was a cousin of the Ch'i Emperor Kao Ti and claimed descent in the twenty third generation from Liu Pang the first emperor of the Han Dynasty seven hundred years earlier. The Emperor Kao Tsu was killed in battle in 549 A.D. when the Toba prince Hou Ching captured Nanking, the capital. His son T'ai Tsung was placed on the throne by Hou Ching as a puppet while another son, Hsiao Yüan, was secretly enthroned by a party of loyalists. In 551 A.D. a Chinese army defeated and executed Hou Ching, deposing T'ai Tsung who died almost certainly violently six weeks later. Hsiao Yüan was enthroned for a second time, this time openly and ruled for three more years. His successor was his ninth son Ching Ti, indicating either a very high infant mortality rate or the previous emperor's determination to allow none to live who could be a threat to his throne. Ching Ti became Emperor at the age of twelve, was forced to abdicate two years later and died at the age of fifteen. He was the last emperor of a short but eventful dynasty.

THE EMPEROR KAO TSU 502 A.D. - 549 A.D.

Five varieties of Wu Chu coins belong to this reign.

No.42. Legend. WU CHU (Five Chus)
(Note. A coin with outer and inner rims on both sides, the only Wu Chu coin so issued. They were called ' Male ' cash.)

No.43. Legend. WU CHU (Five Chus)
(Note. These coins lacked outer and inner rims on both sides. They were called ' Female ' cash.)

No.44. Legend. WU CHU (Five Chus)
(Note. Rather small coins with the legend crowded into the small space between the aperture and the outer edge. These were called ' Immature ' cash and may be compared with the ' Elm Leaf ' issue of Pan Liangs, No.2.)

No.45. Legend. WU CHU (Five Chus)
(Note. Part of the character Chu is missing. They were so issued to discourage clipping the coinage which was prevalent at the time.)

No.46. Legend. WU CHU (Five Chus)
(Note. This Wu Chu is made of iron and is easily distinguishable from those issued by the rebel leader Kung Shun Shi, No.22., by the rounded diagonal strokes of the character Wu and also by the short diagonal rays radiating from the corners of the reverse aperture. The illustration shows the reverse. These coins were issued in 523 A.D. but before the reign ended the rising price of iron precluded its use for coinage.)

No.47. Legend. TA CHI WU CHU (Good Fortune, Five Chus)
(Note. This coin, also issued in 523 A.D. has similar strokes on the reverse as appear on the iron Wu Chu, No. 46)

No.48. Legend. TA FU WU CHU (Great Riches, Five Chus)
(Note. The reverse of this coin resembles the two previous ones. This coin is known only from a coin mould in Taipei Museum, no examples having been found. The illustration shows what the coin would look like, the mirror image of the mould.)

No.49. Legend. TA T'UNG WU CHU (Great coin, Five Chus)
(Note. This coin was issued in both copper and iron, with two iron coins equalling one copper one, a rate of exchange which so favoured counterfeiting that in a short time money lost all its value. The legend, in seal script, includes the period title, Ta T'ung, in use from 527 A.D. to 529 A.D. but it is probable that its inclusion is merely fortuitous.)

THE EMPEROR CHING TI 555 A.D. - 557 A.D.

No.50. Legend. WU CHU (Five Chus)
(Note. The Wu Chu coins of this issue are distinguished by the two dots which appear above and below the obverse aperture. They are known as ' Pillar Cash ')

PERIOD T'AI P'ING 556 A.D. - 557 A.D.

No.51. Legend. T'AI P'ING PAI CHU (One hundred Chus of the Heavenly

Realm.)

THE CH'ÊN DYNASTY 557 A.D. - 589 A.D.

Ch'en Pa Hsien, a general serving in Eastern China, declared himself Emperor in 557 A.D. and took for his title the almost customary Kao Tsu. His realm, the last to rule South China in the period of the Division between the North and the South, was confined to the lower Yangtse valley and after inept rule from no fewer than five emperors in thirty years fell to the Sui Dynasty without serious opposition. The reign of Hsiao Hsüan Ti, a usurper who deposed Fei Ti in 568 A.D., was by far the longest, thirteen years and seven years after his death his son Hou Chu abdicated and the dynasty came to an end.

THE EMPEROR HSIAO HSÜAN TI 569 A.D. - 582 A.D.

No.52. Legend. T'AI HUO LIU CHU (Great coin, six Chus)
(Note. Issued in 579 A.D. this coin was proclaimed to be worth ten Wu Chu coins. As its weight equalled that of the Wu Chu coin this was not feasible and soon its value was declared to be equal to that of the more common coin. Three years later it was withdrawn from circulation.)

THE NORTHERN WEI DYNASTY 386 A.D. - 534 A.D.

This dynasty is perhaps better known as the Toba (or Topa) Tartars. Originally a group of nomadic tribes of Turkish origin living in North Shan-Hsi they allied themselves with Mongol and Tungus tribesmen to form a formidable military alliance. A series of conquests, the Hsien-pi in 409 A.D., the Hsia Kingdom in 431 A.D. and the Northern Liang realms in 439 A.D. brought them to a position of pre-eminence in North China and in 450 A.D. their southern boundary lay along the Yangtse. Their first capital city was Cheng Ting in Chih-Li but as their conquests grew Lo-Yang itself became their first city. By incorporating into their service the Chinese gentry of their realms they produced eventually a society indistinguishable from the native Chinese dynasties and when in 477 A.D. they produced their first coinage it was the typical Chinese cash. This was in the reign of the Emperor Hsiao Wên Ti who ruled North China from 471 A.D. to 499 A.D. He claimed descent from the legendary Yellow Emperor, Huang Ti, of the third millenium B.C. and still further to emphasise that the dynasty was Chinese rather than Tartar altered the family name from Toba to Yüan in 496 A.D.

THE EMPEROR HSIAO WÊN TI 471 A.D. - 499 A.D.
PERIOD T'AI HO 477 A.D. - 499 A.D.

No.53. Legend. T'AI HO WU CHU (Five Chus of Great Harmony)
On the death of Hsiao Wên Ti his son and grandson ruled North China but issued no coins. Then in 528 A.D. a cousin Hsiao Chuang Ti became Emperor and produced the second and last issue of coins attributable to this dynasty. They were first issued in 529 A.D. and some coins bear on the reverse the character T'U alluding to the House of Toba, in Chinese T'U T'E WANG. This coin was also issued by the last four Emperors of the Dynasty - Tung Hai Wang 530 A.D. - 531 A.D., Ch'ien Fei Ti 531 A.D. - 532 A.D., Hou Fei Ti 531 A.D. - 532 A.D. (in opposition to his uncle Ch'ien Fei Ti) and Hsiao Wu 532 A.D. - 534 A.D. - but there is nothing on the coins to distinguish their issues from the 529 A.D. issue. These rapidly changing Emperors are indicative of the disarray into which

the dynasty fell when firm leadership was not forthcoming and in 534 A.D. it fragmented into smaller dynasties.

THE EMPEROR HSIAO CHUANG TI 528 A.D. - 530 A.D.
PERIOD YUNG AN 528 A.D. - 530 A.D.

No.54. Legend. YUNG AN WU CHU (Five Chus of Eternal Peace)

THE NORTHERN CH'I DYNASTY 550 A.D. - 577 A.D.

This dynasty represents one of the fragments of the Toba Dynasty and was founded by the Kao family, formerly from the Hsien-pi. Kao Yang became the first emperor with the title of Wên Hsüan Ti in 550 A.D. and made Chang Tê in Ho-Nan his capital city. The only coin associated with this dynasty was produced in 553 A.D. and the legend is written in seal script. The feeble grasp of the rulers of this dynasty is shown by the fact that of the five Emperors who followed Wên Hsüan Ti on the throne two abdicated, two were deposed and the fifth died within a year of enthronement.

EMPEROR WÊN HSÜAN TI 550 A.D. - 559 A.D.

No.55. Legend. CH'ANG P'ING WU CHU (Five Chus of Constant Standard.)

THE NORTHERN CHOU DYNASTY 557 A.D. - 581 A.D.

This dynasty, the Hsien-pi Tartars, was one of the remnants of the Toba Empire, into which it had been incorporated by conquest in 409 A.D. As with the Toba power rested to a great extent with the Chinese gentry who provided the know-how of government and after several assassinations the Chinese Yang family held the chief positions at court. A member of this family, Yang Chien, organised the massacre of the remnants of the royal family in 581 A.D. and declared himself Emperor, the first of the short lived Sui line.

The first coinage associated with this Northern Chou Dynasty was issued in 561 A.D. by the Emperor Wu Ti who had succeeded to the throne in 560 A.D. on the death of his brother Ming Ti, the first emperor of the Dynasty. The coins issued were Pu Ch'üans, reminiscent of the issue made by the Usurper Wang Mang (See No. 20). These coins were issued for a period of fifteen years and in 575 A.D. a Ta Pu (Great Coin) was issued to circulate at a rate of ten Pu Ch'üans equalling one Ta Pu. China was not ready for a token coinage and the issue was discontinued after a year.

THE EMPEROR WU TI 560 A.D. - 578 A.D.

No.56. Legend. PU CH'ÜAN (Current Coin)
(Note. The centre stroke of the character CH'ÜAN is unbroken, the feature distinguishing this issue from that of Wang Mang, No.20.)

No.57. Legend. WU HSING TA PU (Great Coin of the Five Elements)
(Note. To the Chinese the five elements were...Air, Metal, Fire, Water and Earth.)

When Wu Ti died in 578 A.D. he was succeeded by his son Hsüan Ti who abdicated after a reign of ten months in favour of his eldest son Ching Ti. Ching Ti, the last emperor of the dynasty ruled for two years before he fell to Yang Chien and was in desperate straits for money. Yet another attempt was made to introduce a token coinage by the issue of Wan Kuos which were to circulate as equalling ten of the Pu Ch'üans, but as their weight was barely twice that of the smaller coin the attempt was doomed to failure. So the year 580 A.D. saw not only their issue but also their withdrawal.

THE EMPEROR CHING TI 579 A.D. - 581 A.D.

No.58. Legend. YUNG T'UNG WAN KUO (Everlasting Coin of the Empire)

THE SUI DYNASTY 581 A.D. - 618 A.D.

As mentioned in the previous section, this dynasty was founded by Yang Chien, Duke of Sui, by murder and intrigue. Taking the title of Wên Ti he was enthroned in March 581 A.D., though some histories give the year 589 A.D., the date of the final suppression of the Hsien-pi, as the initial date of the dynasty. Be that as it may the Sui Dynasty saw China reunited after the long divisions between the North and the South and Wên Ti started vigorously to build a system of canals between the Yangtse and Yellow rivers. The ever increasing taxation and enforced labour of the canal building projects made this dynasty unpopular, and its stability was not helped by the murder of Wên Ti by his son Yang Ti in the year 604 A.D. This gentleman ruled for thirteen years before being deposed by his grandson Kung Ti and the following year he was murdered. Kung Ti was deposed after a reign of six months and murdered the following year, when China came under the T'ang Dynasty and order was restored. Chinese history, like that of any other civilisation is marred by dynastic murders, but no dynasty can match the violent record of the Sui Dynasty, three Emperors all of whom were murdered. So an Empire founded by murder perished the same way.

The only coinage associated with this dynasty was an issue of Wu Chus in the first year of his reign by the Emperor Wên Ti. This, the last issue of a coin which had served the commercial needs of the Chinese Empire for over seven centuries, was made of an alloy which contained a high proportion of tin, earning them the name ' White Cash '.

THE EMPEROR WÊN TI 581 A.D. - 604 A.D.

No.59. Legend. WU CHU (Five Chus)
(Note. This issue of Wu Chus can be distinguished by two features -
(a) the light colour caused by a high percentage of tin in the alloy.
(b) the diagonal strokes of the character Wu are straight.

THE T'ANG DYNASTY 618 A.D. - 907 A.D.

Li Yüan, one of the leaders of the revolt against the Sui Dynasty, was the first emperor of the T'ang Dynasty, taking the name Kao Tsu and making Lo-yang in Ho-Nan his capital city. This dynasty is regarded as one of the 'Golden Ages' of Chinese history as art and literature flourished and freed from the threat of invasion from the north the Chinese Empire expanded into Annam, Hanoi being built by a Chinese governor in 767 A.D. While no fewer than twenty three emperors belonged to this dynasty, twenty five reigns as two of them regained the throne after being deposed, Chung Tsung and Jui Tsung, the number of coins issued was only a dozen, the result of the great success enjoyed by the initial issue of coins in 621 A.D. In this year Kao Tsu issued the K'ai Yüans with a weight of ten to the ounce (Liang), that is about two and a half Chu each (about three grams). So successful was its reception by traders and common people alike that for three centuries it was issued time and again by all the rulers of this dynasty, the various issues being indistinguishable except that made by the Emperor Wu Tsung (841 A.D.) and his successors as these bear mint names on the reverse.

These K'ai Yüan coins bring us to an interesting feature of Chinese coinage of this period, the appearance on the reverse of variously placed crescents and dots. The crescent is sometimes explained as being the result of the mould being tested for hardness by a finger nail and sometimes as representing Yüan meaning ' First ', the first year of a reign. Since nothing representing the second or subsequent years has been found I feel that these explanations are wide of the mark. I think that the crescent does represent Yüan but with a meaning of ' Source ' or the chief mint at Lo-yang and the various placing of dots indicate which provincial mint produced the coin. As there is no way of ever discovering the exact meaning of these marks they may be regarded as indicating various moulds and perhaps various mints. I have not listed the many varieties known as these would fill several pages to no useful purpose.

THE EMPEROR KAO TSU 618 A.D. - 626 A.D.

No.60. Legend. K'AI YÜAN T'UNG PAO (Coinage of the Inauguration)
(Notes. (a) Some very rare iron examples are known, probably unofficial.
(b) Coins with a reverse mint name belong to No.70.
(c) For a coin with this legend written in seal script see No. 302)

The second issue of coins associated with this dynasty was made in the year 666 A.D. by the Emperor Kao Tsung, a grandson of the founder of the dynasty. These coins were intended to equal ten of the K'ai Yüan coins but with a weight less than twice the smaller coin it was doomed to failure and the issue was discontinued the same year.

THE EMPEROR KAO TSUNG 649 A.D. - 683 A.D.
PERIOD CH'IEN FÊNG 666 A.D. - 668 A.D.

No.61. Legend. CH'IEN FÊNG CH'ÜAN PAO (Coinage of Celestial Protection)
(Note. Coins with this legend were also issued by the Rebel Prince of Ch'u about 930 A.D. (See No. 339). These however are very much larger pieces, so no confusion can arise.)

A further century was to pass before the next innovation in the coinage, made by the Emperor Su Tsung. This Emperor came to the throne in unusual circumstances as his father abdicated in his favour to escape the consequences of a popular revolt brought on by his extravagances over a lady of the court, Yang Kwei Fei. To save his life Hsüan Tsung, 712 A.D. - 756 A.D., sacrificed the lady and handed over the throne to his third son Su Tsung. The latter using foreign mercenaries suppressed the revolt and prevented the T'ang Dynasty from ending. The coinage introduced in 758 A.D. was a Chung Pao, a Heavy Coin, and was intended to equal fifty of the K'ai Yüans. Being very much under weight it was an open invitation to counterfeiters and so well did they avail themselves of their opportunity that the coin was withdrawn almost as soon as it was issued and replaced by a smaller coin which was given the value of thirty K'ai Yuans. The same results followed and the following year it was re-issued in normal size at a parity with the K'ai Yuans. The sizes are set out below, but it is worth examining these pieces closely as with each reduction in size the opportunity was taken of clipping the larger piece to the size of the smaller, the surplus metal being clear profit. These clipped pieces are easily distinguished as though the rim is smaller the centre portion bearing the legend is unaltered. These Chung Paos were produced in the mint at Yen-chau in Shan-Tung and some pieces bear the mint name of that town on the reverse.

THE EMPEROR SU TSUNG 756 A.D. - 762 A.D.
PERIOD. CH'IEN YÜAN 758 A.D. - 760 A.D.

Nos. 62 - 64. Legend CH'IEN YÜAN CHUNG PAO (Heavy Coin of Celestial Source)

No. 62. Diameter 35 mms. Issued 758 A.D. To equal fifty K'ai Yüans.
No. 63. Diameter 30 mms. Issued 758 A.D. To equal thirty K'ai Yüans.
No. 64. Diameter 24 mms. Issued 759 A.D. To equal one K'ai Yüan.

On the death of Su Tsung in 762 A.D. the throne devolved to his eldest son T'ai Tsung. One coin was issued by this Emperor.

THE EMPEROR T'AI TSUNG 762 A.D. - 779 A.D.
PERIOD TA LI 766 A.D. - 779 A.D.

No. 65. Legend. TA LI YÜAN PAO (Coinage of the Great Succession)

Once again the eldest son succeeded his father on the throne and in 779 A.D. Tê Tsung became Emperor. Two coins are associated with this reign, another attempt to introduce a token coinage and a normal sized cash. The attempted token coinage was an issue of very large K'ai Yüans from the mint of Lien Chou in Kuang-Tung in 780 A.D. These were intended to circulate at a value of ten K'ai Yüans, but with a weight of barely eight of the normal cash the attempt once again failed, and the period of issue was very short, less than one year.

THE EMPEROR TÊ TSUNG 779 A.D. - 805 A.D.

No. 66. Legend. K'AI YÜAN T'UNG PAO (Coinage of the Inauguration) (Note. The largest K'ai Yüan with a diameter of forty mms. Easily distinguishable)

PERIOD CHIEN CHUNG 780 A.D. - 784 A.D.

No. 67. Legend. CHIEN CHUNG T'UNG PAO (Coinage of Moderate Power.)

The next issue of coinage of the T'ang Dynasty, though it must be remembered that the K'ai Yüans were produced reign after reign, was that of the Emperor Mu Tsung, a great grandson of Tê Tsung.

THE EMPEROR MU TSUNG 820 A.D. - 824 A.D.
PERIOD CH'ANG CH'ING 821 A.D. - 824 A.D.

No. 68. Legend. CH'ANG CH'ING T'UNG PAO (Coinage of Everlasting Benevolence)

When Mu Tsung died in 824 A.D. his eldest son Ching Tsung was enthroned. The coinage associated with this reign brings for the first time an interesting point, the repetition of a character in the legend. Such a repetition was considered improper by the Chinese and always arouses doubts as to the authenticity of such pieces. We shall see that in the Sung Dynasty great efforts were made to avoid such improper repetitions.

THE EMPEROR CHING TSUNG 824 A.D. - 827 A.D.
PERIOD PAO LI 824 A.D. - 827 A.D.

No.69. Legend. PAO LI T'UNG PAO (Coinage of the Valued Years)

Ching Tsung was succeeded on the throne by two brothers, Wên Tsung 827 A.D. - 840 A.D. and Wu Tsung 840 A.D. - 846 A.D. During the latter's reign the mint name of the town producing the K'ai Yüans was first placed on the reverse of the coins, a practice continued by his successors on the throne until the end of the T'ang Dynasty. So a K'ai Yüan bearing a mint name on the reverse can belong to any one of six reigns, and until it is discovered when each mint commenced and ceased operating it is not possible to assign these coins to a particular reign. The reigns which used reverse mint names are as follows -

Emperor Wu Tsung 841 A.D. - 847 A.D.
Emperor Hsüan Tsung 847 A.D. - 860 A.D.
Emperor I Tsung 860 A.D. - 874 A.D.
Emperor Hsi Tsung 874 A.D. - 889 A.D.
Emperor Chao Tsung 889 A.D. - 905 A.D.
Emperor Ai Tsung 905 A.D. - 907 A.D.

The following nineteen mint names are to be found on the reverses of these coins ......

1. Chen-Kiang in Chiang-Su
2. Ching-chao in Ho-Nan
3. Ching-chou in Hu-Pei
4. Feng-hsiang in Shan-Hsi
5. Hsiang-chou in Chih-Li
6. Hsi-ch'uan in Ssu-Ch'uan
7. Kwang-chao in Kuang-Tung
8. Kwang-Te in An-Hui
9. Lan-tien in Shan-Hsi
10. Liang-chau in Hu-Pei
11. Lin-Kiang in Chiang-Hsi
12. Lo-yang in Ho-Nan
13. T'an Yang in Hu-Nan
14. Tung-chau in Shen-Hsi
15. Tung-ch'uan in Ssu-Ch'uan
16. Wu-chang in Hu-Pei
17. Yen-chau in Shan-Tung
18. Yu-chau in Che-chiang
19. Yung-ping in Chih-Li.

THE EMPEROR WU TSUNG 840 A.D. - 846 A.D.
(and his successors)

No.70. Legend. K'AI YÜAN T'UNG PAO (Coinage of the Inauguration)

Wu Tsung was succeeded on the throne by a younger brother, Hsüan Tsung, and on his death in 859 A.D. his eldest son I Tsung became Emperor. In his reign was issued the last coin of the T'ang Dynasty.

THE EMPEROR I TSUNG 859 A.D. - 873 A.D.
PERIOD HSIEN T'UNG 860 A.D. - 873 A.D.

No.71. Legend. HSIEN T'UNG LI PAO (Established Coinage of Great Unity)

(Note. The careful use of Li Pao in the legend instead of the more usual T'UNG Pao to avoid the repetition considered incorrect by the Chinese does cast doubts on the authenticity of No.69 where the character PAO is repeated.)

THE EPOCH OF THE FIVE DYNASTIES 907 A.D. - 960 A.D.

Between the fall of the T'ang Dynasty and the rise of the Northern Sung Dynasty China was misruled by a succession of thirteen Emperors divided into five dynasties. The longest reign was only seven years and no fewer than ten out of the thirteen Emperors reigned no more than two years. Seven different coins were issued by these dynasties and all may be considered rare pieces.

THE LATER LIANG DYNASTY 907 A.D. - 922 A.D.

This dynasty, sometimes called Posterior Liang, was founded by Chu Ch'üan-chung who was of peasant origin. After murdering the last T'ang Emperor Chu Ch'üan-chung took the throne with the title T'ai Tsu but the Dynasty was from the very beginning unstable. It was threatened from the north by Turkish tribes led by Li K'o-yung and internally it was faced by intrigue by the Chinese gentry, many of whom had been massacred by T'ai Tsu.

THE EMPEROR T'AI TSU 907 A.D. - 912 A.D.
PERIOD K'AI P'ING 907 A.D. - 911 A.D.

No.72. Legend. K'AI P'ING T'UNG PAO (Coinage of the Coming Peace)

THE LATER T'ANG DYNASTY 923 A.D. - 935 A.D.

This dynasty, also known as the Posterior T'ang Dynasty was founded in North China by Chuang Tsung, the son of Li K'o-yung the enemy of the Later Liang rulers. The policy of the Later Liang dynasty of massacring the Chinese gentry drove them to support this alien dynasty and so give to it the stability due to experienced administration. In the year 936 A.D. the Turkish prince Shih Ching-t'ang succeeded his father-in-law on the throne and altered the dynastic title to the Later Chin. The only coin issued by a ruler of this dynasty was that of the Emperor Ming Tsung, an adopted son of the founder of the dynasty.

THE EMPEROR MING TSUNG 926 A.D. - 935 A.D.
PERIOD T'IEN CH'ÊNG 926 A.D. - 933 A.D.

No.73. Legend. T'IEN CH'ÊNG YÜAN PAO (Coinage of Heavenly Perfection)

THE LATER CHIN DYNASTY 936 A.D. - 947 A.D.

This dynasty, in reality a continuation of the preceding one, was founded by a Turkish prince Shih Ching-t'ang with the assistance of the Kitan tribesmen (See under the Liao Dynasty No. 314 et seq.) Within a decade the price paid for this assistance was first his capital city and shortly after his realms. Shih Ching-t'ang took for his title Kao Tsu and issued two coins.

THE EMPEROR KAO TSU 936 A.D. - 942 A.D.
PERIOD T'IEN FU 936 A.D. - 942 A.D.

No.74. Legend. T'IEN FU YÜAN PAO (Coinage of Heavenly Happiness)
No.75. Legend. T'IEN FU CHÊN PAO (Regal Coinage of Heavenly Happiness)

THE LATER HAN DYNASTY 947 A.D. - 951 A.D.

The Sha-t'o general Liu Chih-yüan gathered families opposed to the Kitan (the Liao Dynasty, see No.314 et seq.) and founded the Later Han Dynasty taking the title Kao Tsu. His success in doing this was only made possible by the death of the Kitan emperor and the subsequent confusion enabled this short lived dynasty to be set up. Kao Tsu died in 948 A.D. and his son, the prisoner of court intrigue, lost his throne to Kuo Wei, a

Chinese general who founded the Later Chou Dynasty. The only coin associated with this dynasty was issued by the founder who besides taking the same title as the founder of the Later Chin dynasty for some reason or other also chose the same period title, T'ien Fu. Hence the legend on his coins.

THE EMPEROR KAO TSU 947 A.D. - 948 A.D.
PERIOD T'IEN FU 947 A.D. - 948 A.D.

No.76. Legend. HAN YÜAN T'UNG PAO (Coinage of the Rising Han)

THE LATER CHOU DYNASTY 951 A.D. - 960 A.D.

This dynasty, also known as the Posterior Chou, was founded in 951 A.D. by a Chinese general Kuo Wei who took as his title T'ai Tsu. One coin is known from this dynasty and since it was extensively copied as an amulet it is the commonest piece from this epoch. On the reverse of some of these 'amulet' coins appear a turtle, a serpent and the Great Bear or Dipper and it is likely that many of such pieces date from much later than the tenth century.

On the reverse of some of the coins issued during the reign of T'ai Tsu appears the mint name of Shun-tien in Chih-Li. The legend closely resembles that of the coins of the preceding dynasty.

THE EMPEROR T'AI TSU 951 A.D. - 954 A.D.
PERIOD KUANG SHUN 951 A.D. - 954 A.D.

No.77. Legend. CHOU YÜAN T'UNG PAO (Coinage of the Rising Chou)

With the deposition of Kung Ti an adopted grandson of T'ai Tsu in 960 A.D. China moved from the anarchy of division into the more settled times of the Sung Dynasty. However the enemy to the north, the nomadic tribesmen of Mongolia and Manchuria, were massing their strength and the peace of China depended on firm leadership from the Sung emperors and when this failed that peace would be of short duration.

THE SUNG DYNASTIES. NORTH AND SOUTH. 960 A.D. - 1279 A.D.

In the year 960 A.D. Chao Kuang Yin, a General in the armies of the Later Chou Dynasty, availed himself of the opportunity afforded him by an army being gathered to oppose the Kitans (Liao Dynasty) to seize the imperial throne and declare himself Emperor with the title of T'ai Tsu. The dynastic capital was Kai-feng in Ho-Nan but pressure from the Kitans and later from the Yüan deprived the dynasty of more and more territory in North China until in 1127 A.D. the Emperor Ch'in Tsung fell prisoner and the capital was transferred to Han-kau in South China. Historians label the period up to this point the Northern Sung Dynasty and the succeeding years until the pathetic Emperor Wei Wang was drowned in a river at Ai Shan by his prime minister to prevent his falling into the hands of the victorious Yüan forces the Southern Sung Dynasty. The division is an artificial one as a glance at the following table of Emperors will show. It is better to consider the period 960 A.D - 1279 A.D. as being the Sung Dynasty.

TABLE OF EMPERORS OF THE SUNG DYNASTY.

	Name.	Enthroned.	Details.
(1)	T'ai Tsung	960 A.D.	Died 976 A.D.
(2)	T'ai Tsung	976 A.D.	Brother of (1) Died 997 A.D.
(3)	Chên Tsung	997 A.D.	Son of (2) Died 1022 A.D.

Name.	Enthroned.	Details.
(4) Jên Tsung	1022 A.D.	Son of (3). Died 1063 A.D.
(5) Ying Tsung	1063 A.D.	Great grandson of (2) Died 1067 A.D.
(6) Shên Tsung	1067 A.D.	Son of (5) Died 1085 A.D.
(7) Chê Tsung	1085 A.D.	Son of (6) Died 1100 A.D.
(8) Hui Tsung	1100 A.D.	Son of (6) Abdicated 1126 A.D. Died 1135 A.D.
(9) Ch'in Tsung	1126 A.D.	Son of (8) Prisoner 1127 A.D. Died 1161 A.D.

(Here is the traditional division between North and South Sung.)

(10) Kao Tsung	1127 A.D.	Son of (8) Abdicated 1162 A.D. Died 1187 A.D.
(11) Hsiao Tsung	1162 A.D.	Descended from (1) Abdicated 1189 A.D. Died 1194 A.D.
(12) Kuang Tsung	1189 A.D.	Son of (11) Abdicated 1194 A.D. Died 1200 A.D.
(13) Ning Tsung	1194 A.D.	Son of (12) Died 1224 A.D.
(14) Li Tsung	1224 A.D.	Descended from (1) Died 1264 A.D.
(15) Tu Tsung	1264 A.D.	Nephew of (15) Died 1274 A.D.
(16) Kung Tsung	1274 A.D.	Son of (15). Prisoner 1276 A.D.
(17) Tuan Tsung	1276 A.D.	Son of (15). Died 1278 A.D.
(18) Wei Wang	1278 A.D.	Son of (15). Drowned 1279 A.D.

The Sung Dynasty produced a prolific coinage as of the eighteen Emperors who ruled China during this time only the last two did not issue coins, understandably enough in the conditions then prevailing. Practically every Year Period saw the issue of a new series of coins and the number for the collector is greatly increased by the use of varying styles of writing used in the legends, coins with the legend reading both clockwise and the normal order, the use of two metals, iron and copper alloy, the appearance of numerous mint names and finally the practice adopted by many Emperors of adding on the reverse a numeral indicating the year of issue. Altogether this Dynasty will provide the collector with a great deal of material, most of it quite easily obtained as the coins were cast by the millions to meet the increasing commercial needs of China. It is difficult to obtain the iron coins in anything like collectable condition and some types are rare but most of the copper alloy issues are commonly met with.

THE EMPEROR T'AI TSU 960 A.D. - 976 A.D.
PERIOD K'AI PAO 968 A.D. - 976 A.D.

No.78. Legend. SUNG YÜAN T'UNG PAO (Coinage of the Rising Sung.)

(Note. This legend was chosen to avoid the improper repetition of a character which would have occurred had the period title been used.)

THE EMPEROR T'AI TSUNG 976 A.D. - 997 A.D.
PERIOD T'AI P'ING 976 A.D. - 984 A.D.

No.79. Legend. T'AI P'ING T'UNG PAO (Coinage of the Heavenly Kingdom)

(Note. The archaic form of the character Pao distinguished this issue from one with the same legend of the T'ai P'ing rebels in the nineteenth century.)

PERIOD. SHUN HUA 990 A.D. - 995 A.D.

Nos. 80-81. Legend SHUN HUA YÜAN PAO (Coinage of Extensive Honour)

No. 80. Legend written in orthodox characters

No. 81. Legend written in cursive style.

Note. Both coins are read in a clockwise direction.

PERIOD. CHIH TAO 995 A.D. - 997 A.D.

Nos. 82-85. Legend. CHIH TAO YÜAN PAO (Coinage of Perfect Truth)

No. 82. Legend written in seal script.

No. 83. Legend written in orthodox characters

No. 84. Legend written in cursive style.

No. 85. Legend written in ' grass writing '

Note. There are many varieties of the cursive style of writing and No.85 is included to the form known as ' grass writing '. All these coins are read in a clockwise direction.

THE EMPEROR CHÊN TSUNG 997 A.D. - 1023 A.D.
PERIOD. HSIEN P'ING 998 A.D. - 1004 A.D.

No. 86. Legend. HSIEN P'ING YÜAN PAO (Coinage of Celestial Greatness)

Note. The legend is read in a clockwise direction.

PERIOD. CHING TÊ 1004 A.D. - 1008 A.D.

No. 87. Legend. CHING TÊ YÜAN PAO (Coinage of Expected Virtue)
Note. The legend, written in the cursive style, is read in a clockwise direction. The iron coins of this issue exist in two sizes, the larger being equal in value to the copper issue, while the smaller was valued at one tenth of the copper.

PERIOD. HSIANG FU 1008 A.D. - 1017 A.D.

No. 88. Legend. HSIANG FU YÜAN PAO (Coinage of Promised Happiness).

No. 89. Legend. HSIANG FU T'UNG PAO (Coinage of Promised Happiness)

Note. The legends of both coins of this period are read in a clockwise direction.

PERIOD. T'IEN HSI 1017 A.D. - 1022 A.D.

No. 90. Legend. T'IEN HSI T'UNG PAO (Coinage of Celestial Blessing)
Note. The legend of this coin is read in a clockwise direction.
In the Schjöth collection is Oslo there is a coin with this legend where each character is written in a different style, T'IEN in seal script, HSI in orthodox characters, T'UNG in cursive style, and PAO in what is called the ' Official ' style. It is difficult to see how this curiosity could have been issued officially. It is probably the whimsy of a bored mint official.

THE EMPEROR JÊN TSUNG 1022 A.D. - 1063 A.D.
PERIOD T'IEN SHÊNG 1023 A.D. - 1032 A.D.

Nos. 91-92. Legend. T'IEN SHÊNG YÜAN PAO (Coinage of Celestial Holiness)

No. 91. Legend written in seal script.

No. 92. Legend written in orthodox characters.

Note. The legend, in both styles, is read in a clockwise direction.

PERIOD MING PAO 1032 A.D. - 1034 A.D.

Nos. 93-94. Legend MING TAO YÜAN PAO (Coinage of Apparent Truth)

No. 93. Legend written in seal script.
No. 94. Legend written in orthodox characters.
Note. The legend, in both styles, is read in a clockwise direction.

PERIOD CHING YU 1034 A.D. - 1038 A.D.

Nos. 95-96. Legend CHING YU YÜAN PAO (Coinage of Foreseen Rectitude)

No. 95. Legend written in seal script.
No. 96. Legend written in orthodox characters.
Note. The legend, in both styles, is read in a clockwise direction.

PERIOD PAO YÜAN 1038 A.D. - 1040 A.D.

Nos. 97-98. Legend. HUANG SUNG T'UNG PAO (Coinage of the Sung Empire)

No. 97. Legend written in seal script.
No. 98. Legend written in orthodox characters.
Note. This legend was chosen to avoid the improper repetition of characters which would have occurred had the period title been used. The coins written in orthodox characters, No. 98, will be found with both large and small characters in the legend.

PERIOD K'ANG TING 1040 A.D. - 1041 A.D.

No.99. Legend. K'ANG TING YÜAN PAO (Coinage of Settled Peace)
Note. The legend is read in a clockwise direction. With a period of issue of less than a year this coin is rather scarce.

PERIOD CH'ING LI 1041 A.D. - 1049 A.D.

Nos. 100-101. Legend. CH'ING LI CHUNG PAO (Heavy Coinage of the Blessed Line)

No. 100. Legend read in the normal order.
No. 101. Legend read in a clockwise direction.
Note. The Chung Pao coinage circulated at a value of three times that of the current Yüan Pao coinage.

PERIOD HUANG YU 1049 A.D. - 1054 A.D.

No. 102. Legend. HUANG YU YÜAN PAO (Coinage of the Moral Empire)

Note. The legend is read in a clockwise direction.

PERIOD CHIH HO 1054 A.D. - 1056 A.D.

Nos. 103-105. Legend. CHIH HO YÜAN PAO (Coinage of Perfect Harmony)

No. 103. Legend written in seal script.
No. 104. Legend written in orthodox characters.
No. 105. Legend written in the cursive style.
Note. The legend, written in all three styles, is read in a clockwise direction.

Nos. 106-107. Legend. CHIH HO T'UNG PAO (Coinage of Perfect Harmony)

No. 106. Legend written in seal script.

No. 107. Legend written in orthodox characters.

PERIOD CHIA YU 1056 A.D. - 1063 A.D.

Nos. 108 - 109. Legend CHIA YU YÜAN PAO (Coinage of Increasing Right)

No. 108. Legend written in seal script.
No. 109. Legend written in orthodox characters.
Note. The legend, written in both styles, is read in a clockwise direction.

Nos. 110 - 111. Legend. CHIA YU T'UNG PAO (Coinage of Increasing Right)

No. 110. Legend written in seal script.
No. 111 . Legend written in orthodox characters.

THE EMPEROR YING TSUNG 1063 A.D. - 1067 A.D.
PERIOD CHIH P'ING 1064 A.D. - 1067 A.D.

Nos. 112 - 113. Legend. CHIH P'ING YÜAN PAO (Coinage of Healing Peace)

No. 112. Legend written in seal script, many variants.
No. 113. Legend written in orthodox characters.

Nos. 114-115. Legend. CHIH P'ING T'UNG PAO (Coinage of Healing Peace)

No. 114. Legend written in seal script, many variants.
No. 115. Legend written in orthodox characters.

THE EMPEROR SHÊN TSUNG 1067 A.D. - 1085 A.D.
PERIOD HSI NING 1068 A.D. - 1078 A.D.

Nos. 116 - 117. Legend. HSI NING YÜAN PAO (Coinage of Greater Peace)

No. 116. Legend written in seal script.
No. 117. Legend written in orthodox characters.
Note. The legend, written in both styles, is read in a clockwise direction.
No. 118. Legend. HSI NING T'UNG PAO (Coinage of Greater Peace)
Note. The legend is read in a clockwise direction. This legend is not recorded by Ku Ch'üan Hui and the coin is a rare one.

Nos. 119 - 120. Legend. HSI NING CHUNG PAO (Heavy Coinage of Greater Peace)

No. 119. Legend written in seal script.
No. 120. Legend written in orthodox characters.
Note. The legend, in both styles, is read in a clockwise direction.

PERIOD YÜAN FÊNG 1078 A.D. - 1085 A.D.

Nos. 121 - 123. Legend YÜAN FÊNG T'UNG PAO (Coinage of Coming Prosperity)

No. 121. Legend written in seal script.
No. 122. Legend written in orthodox characters.
No. 123. Legend written in cursive style.
Note. The legend, in all three styles, is read in a clockwise direction. There was no Yüan Pao coinage during this period as its use would have entailed an improper repetition in the legend of the coins.

THE EMPEROR CHÊ TSUNG 1085 A.D. - 1100 A.D.
PERIOD YÜAN YU 1086 A.D. - 1094 A.D.

Nos. 124 - 126. Legend YÜAN YU T'UNG PAO (Coinage of Expected

Rectitude)
No. 124. Legend written in seal script.
No. 125. Legend written in orthodox characters.
No. 126. Legend written in cursive style.
Note. The legend, written in all three styles, is read in a clockwise direction. There was no issue of Yüan Pao coinage during this period as its use would have entailed an improper repetition in the legend.

PERIOD SHAO SHÊNG 1094 A.D. - 1098 A.D.

Nos. 127-129. Legend. SHAO SHÊNG YÜAN PAO (Coinage of Sacred Inheritance)

No. 127. Legend written in seal script.
No. 128. Legend written in orthodox characters.
No. 129. Legend written in cursive style.
Note. The legend, in all three styles is read in a clockwise direction. The iron coins of this issue circulated at a rate of five iron coins equalling two copper coins.
No. 130. Legend SHAO SHÊNG T'UNG PAO (Coinage of Sacred Inheritance)

PERIOD YÜAN FU 1098 A.D. - 1100 A.D.

Nos. 131 - 132. Legend. YÜAN FU T'UNG PAO (Coinage of Charmed Beginning)

No. 131. Legend written in seal script.
No. 132. Legend written in cursive style.
Note. The legend, written in both styles, is read in a clockwise direction. There was no issue of Yüan Pao coinage during this period as its use would have entailed the improper repetition of the character Yüan in the legend. It is rather surprising that the Yüan Fu coinage should not include specimens with the legend written in orthodox characters.

THE EMPEROR HUI TSUNG 1100 A.D. - 1126 A.D.
PERIOD CHIEN CHUNG 1101 A.D. - 1102 A.D.

Nos. 133-135. Legend SHÊNG SUNG YÜAN PAO (Coinage of Holy Sung)

No. 133. Legend written in seal script.
No. 134. Legend written in orthodox characters.
No. 135. Legend written in the cursive style.
No. 136. Legend. SHÊNG SUNG T'UNG PAO (Coinage of Holy Sung)
Note. See No. 175 for a coin reading SHÊNG SUNG CHUNG PAO.

PERIOD CH'UNG NING 1102 A.D. - 1107 A.D.

No. 137. Legend. CH'UNG NING YÜAN PAO (Coinage of Greater Reverence)
No. 138. Legend. CH'UNG NING T'UNG PAO (Coinage of Greater Reverence)
No. 139. Legend. CH'UNG NING CHUNG PAO (Heavy Coinage of Greater Reverence)
Note. No. 138 is the only one of this period whose legend is read in a clockwise direction, the other two being read in the normal manner.

PERIOD TA KUAN 1107 A.D. - 1111 A.D.

No. 140. Legend TA KUAN T'UNG PAO (Coinage of Visible Greatness)

PERIOD CHÊNG HO 1111 A.D. - 1118 A.D.

Nos. 141 - 142. Legend. CHÊNG HO T'UNG PAO. (Coinage of Official Harmony)

No. 141. Legend written in seal script.
No. 142 Legend written in orthodox characters.
No. 143. Legend CHÊNG HO CHUNG PAO (Heavy Coinage of Official Harmony)

PERIOD CH'UNG HO 1118 A.D. - 1119 A.D.

No. 144. Legend. CH'UNG HO T'UNG PAO (Coinage of Great Harmony)

PERIOD HSÜAN HO 1119 A.D. - 1126 A.D.

No. 145. Legend HSÜAN HO YÜAN PAO (Coinage of Proclaimed Harmony)

Note. The legend on this coin is read in a clockwise direction.

Nos. 146 - 147. Legend HSÜAN HO T'UNG PAO (Coinage of Proclaimed Harmony)

No. 146. Legend is written in seal script.
No. 147. Legend is written in orthodox characters.
Note. Some of the T'ung Pao coinage have on the reverse the mint name of Shen-Hsi Province, the first use of a mint name by this dynasty.

THE EMPEROR CH'IN TSUNG 1126 A.D. - 1127 A.D.
PERIOD CHING K'ANG 1126 A.D. - 1127 A.D.

Nos. 148 - 149. Legend CHING K'ANG YÜAN PAO (Coinage of Pleasing Prosperity)

No. 148. Legend is written in seal script.
No. 149. Legend is written in orthodox characters.

Nos. 150 - 151. Legend. CHING K'ANG T'UNG PAO (Coinage of Pleasing Prosperity)

No. 150. Legend is written in seal script.
No. 151. Legend is written in orthodox characters.
Note. The coins of this short reign are rare. As mentioned previously this Emperor fell into the hands of the Nu Chên Tartars in 1127 A.D. and this date is recognised as the end of the Northern Sung Dynasty and the start of the Southern portion of the Sung Dynasty. Ch'in Tsung died in prison in 1161 A.D. In the meantime his brother Kao Tsung had escaped to the south and re-established the dynasty with Nan-king as capital. When this city fell to the Tartar armies the capital was transferred to Han-kau. The city of Nan-king was recaptured by the Chinese using a fleet of ships but though another one hundred and fifty years were to pass before the whole of China came under alien rule the Southern Sung fought a losing battle. Once the grain lands of the north and the trade routes to Central Asia fell into the hands of the Tartars and their successors the Yüan there could be only one ending to this portion of China's story. In 1160 A.D. the Tarters made their last attempt to conquer South China but the line of the Yangtse was held and this threat faded. However this dynasty proved that they had learned nothing from the history of China by forming an alliance with the Mongols against the Tartars. In 1234 A.D. the Tartars were conquered and the Mongols turned their armies against their allies. Forty years of intermittent warfare followed but slowly the Chinese armies were forced further and further to the

south until the last Emperor of the Sungs was killed to prevent him falling a prisoner to the Mongols. The Mongol Dynasty, the Yüan, thus became the first alien dynasty to rule all China.

During the second half of the Sung Dynasty the coinage followed a similar pattern to that of the Northern portion of the Dynasty with two differences... (a) the scarcity of copper made the use of iron more widespread in the coinage and (b) three values of cash were issued, namely one, two and three cash, weighing respectively three, six and nine grams. Even during the reigns of the last few emperors when the pressure from the advancing Mongols brought about the disintegration of many aspects of Chinese life these standards of weight were maintained.

THE EMPEROR KAO TSUNG 1127 A.D. - 1162 A.D.
PERIOD CHIEN YEN 1127 A.D. - 1131 A.D.

Nos. 152 - 153. Legend. CHIEN YEN T'UNG PAO (Coinage of Brilliant Strength)

No. 152. Legend is written in seal script.
No. 153. Legend is written in orthodox characters.
Note. Some of the coins with the legend in orthodox characters, No. 153, have on the reverse the mint name of Cheng-tu in Ssu-Ch'uan.

PERIOD SHAO HSING 1131 A.D. - 1162 A.D.

Nos. 154 - 155. Legend. SHAO HSING YÜAN PAO (Coinage of the Prosperous Heritage)

No. 154. Legend written in seal script.
No. 155. Legend written in orthodox characters.
Note. In both styles of writing the legend is read in a clockwise direction.
No. 156. Legend. SHAO HSING T'UNG PAO (Coinage of the Prosperous Heritage)
Note. Some coins of this issue have on the reverse the mint name Li-chao, a district on the borders of Shen-Hsi and Ssu-Ch'uan.
No. 157. Legend. CHAO NA HSIN PAO (Coinage as Proof of Loyalty)
Note. These tokens, they can hardly be called coins, were issued by Liu Kuang Shih, the governor of Hu-Pei as a mark of his allegiance to the Sung Dynasty in the face of the Tartar attacks. Perhaps the date of issue was 1129 A.D. when during a rebellion the Emperor was deposed for some weeks. Sometimes this piece is said to be a coin issued by the leader of the rebel state of Ch'i, Tsao Wang, during this reign. The legend seems somehow more appropriate from a governor than a rebel leader. However the aptness of some of the regal legends during this dynasty is open to debate. The reverse of these coins bear the character SHIH, which seems to me to allude to Liu Kuang Shih himself.

THE EMPEROR HSIAO TSUNG 1162 A.D. - 1189 A.D.
PERIOD LUNG HSING 1162 A.D. - 1165 A.D.

Nos. 158 - 159. Legend. LUNG HSING YÜAN PAO (Coinage of Eminent Prosperity)

No. 158. Legend written in seal script.
No. 159. Legend written in orthodox characters.
Note. Both styles of writing are to be read in a clockwise direction.

PERIOD CH'IEN TAO 1165 A.D. - 1174 A.D.

Nos. 160 - 161. Legend. CH'IEN TAO YÜAN PAO (Coinage of Celestial

Truth)
No. 160. Legend written in seal script.
No. 161. Legend written in orthodox characters.
Note. Both styles of writing are to be read in a clockwise direction. On the reverse of some coins of this issue appears the mint name of Chiung in Ssu-Ch'uan.

PERIOD SHUN HSI 1174 A.D. - 1189 A.D.

Nos. 162-163. Legend. SHUN HSI YÜAN PAO (Coinage of Blessed Purity)
No. 162. Legend is written in seal script.
No. 163. Legend is written in orthodox characters.
Note. Both styles of writing are to be read in a clockwise direction. On the reverse of some of the coins of this issue will be found the mint names of Chi-chun, Chiung District, Li Chao, Tung-an and Yen-chao. This issue commenced in 1180 A.D. and the appropriate number from seven to sixteen on the reverse indicates the year of issue. This is the first time this practice was followed on Chinese coins.
Nos. 164 - 165. Legend. SHUN HSI T'UNG PAO (Coinage of Blessed Purity)
No. 164. The characters of the legend are read in a clockwise direction.
No. 165. The characters of the legend are read in the normal manner, top, bottom, right and left.
Note. As with the issue of Yüan Paos the appropriate number from seven to sixteen indicates the year of issue, the first issue having been made in 1180 A.D.

THE EMPEROR KUANG TSUNG 1189 A.D. - 1194 A.D.
PERIOD SHAO HSI 1189 A.D. - 1194 A.D.

No. 166. Legend. SHAO HSI YÜAN PAO (Coinage of the Settled Heritage)
Note. The legend is read in a clockwise direction. On the reverse appears the appropriate number from one to five to indicate the year of issue, the character YÜAN replacing YI for one. The following mint names appear on the coins of this issue. Chi-chun, Han-yang and Tung-an.
No. 167. Legend SHAO HSI T'UNG PAO (Coinage of the Settled Heritage)
Note. This legend is written in seal script and as the coins were issued from the mint at Chi-chun that mint name, also written in seal script is to be found on the reverse of many coins of this issue.

THE EMPEROR NING TSUNG 1194 A.D. - 1224 A.D.
PERIOD CH'ING YÜAN 1195 A.D. - 1201 A.D.

No. 168. Legend CH'ING YÜAN YÜAN PAO (Coinage of the Fortunate Beginning)
Note. This is a strange issue with the character YÜAN repeated in the legend and the numbers on the reverse do not make sense. Altogether it is difficult to see how this could be an official issue. They appear to have emanated from the mint of Cheng-tu, as that mint name appears on the reverse of some of these 'coins'.
Nos. 169 - 170. Legend. CH'ING YÜAN T'UNG PAO (Coinage of the Fortunate Beginning)
No. 169. Legend read in a clockwise order.
No. 170. Legend read in the normal order, top, bottom, right and left.
Note. The appropriate number from one to six on the reverse indicates

the year of issue, the character YÜAN replacing YI for one. The following mint names are to be found on the reverse of some of the coins of this issue....Chi-chun, Han-yang and Tung-an.

PERIOD CHIA T'AI 1201 A.D. - 1205 A.D.

Nos. 171 - 172. Legend. CHIA T'AI YÜAN PAO (Coinage of Increasing Honour)

No. 171. Characters of legend read in a clockwise direction.

No. 172. Characters of legend read in normal manner, top, bottom, right and left.

Note. The appropriate number from one to four, with YÜAN replacing YI for the initial year, indicate the year of issue. Some coins bear numbers higher than four, these may be counterfeits or possibly mould numbers. The following mint names are found....Cheng-tu, Chi-chun, Han-yang and Li-chao.

Nos. 173 - 174. Legend CHIA T'AI T'UNG PAO (Coinage of Increasing Honour)

No. 173. Characters of legend read in a clockwise direction.

No. 174. Characters of legend read in the normal manner, top, bottom, right and left.

Note. The appropriate number from one to four, with YÜAN replacing YI for the initial year, indicate the year of issue. The following mint names are to be found...Chi-chun, Han-yang and Tung-an.

PERIOD K'AI HSI 1205 A.D. - 1208 A.D.

No. 175. Legend SHÊNG SUNG CHUNG PAO (Heavy Coinage of the Holy Sung)

Note. These coins, valued at five ordinary cash, were issued in 1205 A.D. and some bear on the reverse the character WU, five. The only mint producing these coins was apparently Li-chao, the name of which is to be found on the reverse of most coins.

See Nos. 133 - 136 for coins with a similar legend.

No. 176. Legend. K'AI HSI YÜAN PAO (Coinage of the Blessed Beginning)

Note. The legend is read in a clockwise direction. As with No. 175 these coins were produced by Li-chao mint in 1205 A.D. and that mint name appears on the reverse of most coins.

No. 177. Legend. K'AI HSI T'UNG PAO (Coinage of the Blessed Beginning)

Note. The legend is read in a clockwise direction. The appropriate number from one to three, with YÜAN, as usual, replacing YI for one, indicates the year of issue. The following three mints produced this issue and their mint names appear on the reverse of the coins.... Chi-chun, Han-yang and Tung-an.

PERIOD CHIA TING 1208 A.D. - 1224 A.D.

Nos. 178 - 180. Legend. CHIA TING YÜAN PAO (Coinage of Increasing Peace)

No. 178. Legend written in seal script and read in a clockwise direction.

No. 179. Legend written in orthodox characters and read in a clockwise direction.

No. 180. Legend written in orthodox characters and read in the normal manner, top, bottom, right and left.

Note. These iron coins were cast at the mint at Li-chao in 1208 A.D. and bear that mint name on the reverse. Copper specimens of this issue are very rare and are probably pattern or trial pieces.

Nos. 181-182. Legend. CHIA TING T'UNG PAO (Coinage of Increasing Peace)

No. 181. Characters read in a clockwise direction.

No. 182. Characters read in the normal manner, top, bottom, right and left.

Note. The appropriate number from one to fourteen, with YÜAN replacing YI for one, indicates the year of issue. Five mints produced this issue and one of the following mint names will be found on the reverse .... Chi-chun, Chuan-hsi, Han-yang, Ting-cheng and Tung-an.

No. 183. Legend. CHIA TING AN PAO (Peaceful Coinage of Increasing Peace)

No. 184. Legend. CHIA TING CHÊN PAO (Genuine Coinage of Increasing Peace)

No. 185. Legend. CHIA TING CHÊN PAO (Valued Coinage of Increasing Peace)

No. 186. Legend. CHIA TING CHÊNG PAO (True Coinage of Increasing Peace)

Note. The legend on this coin is read in a clockwise direction. Copper specimens of this issue are probably patterns or trial pieces.

No. 187. Legend. CHIA TING CHIH PAO (The Very Coinage of Increasing Peace)

Note. The character CHIH indicates the possessive case and is best translated as ' Very '. These coins were cast at the mints at Ch'uan Hsi, Hui-Min and Li Chou and these mint names will be found on the reverse of many of them.

No. 188. Legend. CHIA TING CHIH PAO (Precious Coinage of Increasing Peace)

No. 189. Legend. CHIA TING CH'ÜAN PAO (Perfect Coinage of Increasing Peace)

Nos. 190-191. Legend CHIA TING CHUNG PAO (Heavy Coinage of Increasing Peace)

No. 190. Legend is written in seal script.

No. 191. Legend is written in orthodox characters.

No. 192. Legend. CHIA TING CH'UNG PAO (Noble Coinage of Increasing Peace)

No. 193. Legend. CHIA TING HSIN PAO (New Coinage of Increasing Peace)

Note. The legend of this coin is read in a clockwise direction.

No. 194. Legend. CHIA TING HSING PAO (Prosperous Coinage of Increasing Peace)

No. 195. Legend. CHIA TING HUNG PAO (Great Coinage of Inceasing Peace)

No. 196. Legend. CHIA TING LI PAO (Established Coinage of Increasing Peace)

Note. The legend of this coin is read in a clockwise direction.

No. 197. Legend. CHIA TING WAN PAO (Myriad Coinage of Increasing Peace)

Note. The character WAN strictly translated means ten thousand but as the implication is of a plenteous coinage I have used ' Myriad '.

No. 198. Legend. CHIA TING YUNG PAO (Eternal Coinage of Increasing Peace)

Note. The legend of this coin is read in a clockwise direction. This issue was cast in the mint at Ting-cheng in Kuang-Tung Province and bears that mint name on the reverse.

Notes on the Chia Ting Issue -

There seems to be no valid explanation for the great number of variant legends used during this issue. It is safe to say that with the exception of the YÜAN PAO and T'UNG PAO issues all are very rare and having in most cases been cast in iron it is extremely difficult with a worn specimen to allocate it to its correct position.

THE EMPEROR LI TSUNG 1224 A.D. - 1264 A.D.
PERIOD PAO CH'ING 1225 A.D. - 1227 A.D.

No. 199. Legend PAO CH'ING YÜAN PAO (Coinage of Precious Fortune)
Note. It is difficult to believe that this is an official issue with the character PAO repeated in the legend. A coin mould dated the fifteenth year of the Han Emperor Shih Tsu, i.e. in the year 40 A.D. shows that even at that time there was an official whose function was to inspect the coin moulds before use. I feel that this piece has been made with intent to defraud.

No. 200. Legend. TA SUNG YÜAN PAO (Coinage of Great Sung)
Note. The legend is read in a clockwise direction and on the reverse appears one of the mint names of Chuan-Hsi, Li-chao or Yen-chao. The appropriate number from one to three, with the character YÜAN replacing YI for the initial year of issue, indicates when the coin was cast. The issue of the TA Sung coinage, obviously to avoid using a period title which produced an improper repetition in the legend, would certainly seem to emphasize the doubts cast on No. 199.

PERIOD SHAO TING 1227 A.D. - 1233 A.D.

No. 201. Legend. SHAO TING YÜAN PAO (Coinage of the Calm Heritage)
Nos. 202 - 203. Legend SHAO TING T'UNG PAO (Coinage of the Calm Heritage)
No. 202. The legend is read in a clockwise direction.
No. 203. The legend is read in the normal manner, top, bottom, right and left.
Note. The numbers from one to six are used on the reverse to indicate the year of issue, with YÜAN replacing YI for the initial year, 1228 A.D. Some coins bear the mint name of Chi-chun on the reverse.

PERIOD TUAN P'ING 1234 A.D. - 1237 A.D.

No. 204. Legend TUAN P'ING YÜAN PAO (Coinage of Coming Peace)
Note. The legend is read in a clockwise direction. One of three mint names appears on the reverse ... Chiung, Li-chao and Ting-cheng.

No. 205. Legend. TUAN P'ING T'UNG PAO (Coinage of Coming Peace)
Note. These coins were cast at the mint in Hui-Min, and this mint name appears on the reverse of some of them.
On the reverse of both the YÜAN PAO and T'UNG PAO issues appears the appropriate number from one to three to indicate the year of issue. As usual YÜAN replaces YI for the initial year 1234 A.D.

No. 206. Legend TUAN P'ING CHUNG PAO (Heavy Coinage of Coming Peace)

PERIOD CHIA HSI 1237 A.D. - 1240 A.D.

No. 207. Legend. CHIA HSI T'UNG PAO (Coinage of Increased Calm)
No. 208. Legend. CHIA HSI CHUNG PAO (Heavy Coinage of Increased Calm)

Note. On both the T'UNG PAO and CHUNG PAO issues the reverse bears the appropriate number from one to four, with YÜAN replacing YI for the initial year 1237 A.D. The legend of the CHUNG PAO is read in a clockwise direction.

PERIOD SHUN YU 1240 A.D. - 1252 A.D.

No. 209. Legend SHUN YU YÜAN PAO (Coinage of Protecting Obedience)
Note. The legend is read in a clockwise direction. On the reverse the year of issue is indicated by the appropriate number from one to twelve, with YÜAN replacing YI for the initial year 1231 A.D.

No. 210. Legend SHUN YU T'UNG PAO (Coinage of Protecting Obedience)
Note. These large coins bear on the reverse the value of one hundred cash. As their weight varies between five and ten normal cash they were not acceptable and were soon withdrawn. Their issue is a harbinger of the imminent suppression of the Sung Dynasty by the Mongol invaders.

PERIOD PAO YU 1252 A.D. - 1258 A.D.

No. 211. Legend. HUANG SUNG YÜAN PAO (Coinage of the Sung Empire)

Note. The legend is read in a clockwise direction. The reverse bears the appropriate number from one to six to indicate the year of issue, YÜAN as usual replacing YI for the initial year 1253 A.D. Since the year period title contains the character PAO it could not be used in the legend of the coinage to avoid improper repetition, hence the HUANG SUNG legend.

PERIOD K'AI CH'ING 1259 A.D. - 1260 A.D.

No.212. Legend. K'AI CH'ING T'UNG PAO (Coinage of Coming Prosperity)
Note. The reverse bears the character YÜAN to indicate 1259 A.D., the initial and only year of issue. This is a very rare coin.

PERIOD CHING TING 1260 A.D. - 1264 A.D.

No. 213. Legend. CHING TING YÜAN PAO (Coinage of Settled Circumstances)
Note. The reverse indicates the year of issue with the appropriate number from one to five with YÜAN as usual replacing YI for the initial year 1260 A.D. This is the last coinage of the Emperor Li Tsung. During the course of his reign of forty years the year period title was altered seven times and coins were issued for all eight periods.

THE EMPEROR TU TSUNG 1264 A.D. - 1274 A.D.
PERIOD HSIEN SHUN 1264 A.D. - 1274 A.D.

No. 214. Legend. HSIEN SHUN YÜAN PAO (Coinage of Unmixed Good)
Note. The reverse bears the appropriate number from one to eight to indicate the year of issue, YÜAN replacing YI for the initial year 1265 A.D. No coins have yet been found with either of the numbers nine or ten on the reverse so it must be assumed that production ceased in 1272 A.D.

THE EMPEROR KUNG TSUNG 1274 A.D. - 1276 A.D.
PERIOD TÊ YU 1275 A.D. - 1276 A.D.

No.215. Legend. TÊ YU YÜAN PAO (Coinage of Protective Virtue)

THE EMPEROR TUAN TSUNG 1276 A.D. - 1278 A.D.
THE EMPEROR WEI WANG 1278 A.D. - 1279 A.D.

Note. Neither of these two Emperors, the last of the Sung Dynasty, issued any cash. With the country falling into a state of chaos before the Mongols this is scarcely surprising. However rectangular copper tallies of Lin An Prefecture are known bearing the values five or two hundred cash and these are sometimes assigned to the reign of Wei Wang. They have no period title and since they were most probably nothing more than treasury tallies for accounting purposes I have omitted them.

THE YÜAN DYNASTY 1279 A.D. - 1367 A.D.

This Tartar Dynasty achieved control of all China in 1280 A.D. though with the hindsight of victory their earlier leaders from Gengis Khan, 1206 A.D. - 1227 A.D. were given the rank and titles of Emperor. The first leader of the YÜAN actually to rule as Emperor was the redoubtable Kublai Khan from 1280 A.D. - 1294 A.D., though he had assumed leadership in May 1260 A.D. Below will be found a table of Emperors of this Dynasty which gives their Tartar names as well as the dates etc.

The Sung Dynasty had initiated the use of paper money and the YÜAN Dynasty continued and extended its use. Indeed those Emperors who did issue coins did so in very small quantities, in thousands of cash rather than millions, and most of the coins of this era are very rare. Many of these coins are known from only a single specimen in Taiwan Museum and in the case of No. 232 the only trace of the coin's existence is a reference in one of the old coin manuals. Collectors will find Nos. 221 and 239 of great interest as their legends are written in Mongol, the first Chinese coins whose legends were not written in Chinese. Fortunately both are among the less rare coins of the Dynasty.

This Dynasty also first saw contact made between the civilisations of the East and West as to the court of Kublai Khan in 1276 A.D. came the Venetian traveller and romancer Marco Polo and his account of his wanderings gives us the first outside view of China. Some twenty years after his visit the first missionary from Rome reached China and in 1313 A.D. a Franciscan, John of Montecorvino was consecrated Archbishop of Pekin.

THE EMPERORS OF THE YÜAN DYNASTY
(Mongol names given after the Chinese title)

	Emperor	Enthroned	Details.
(1)	Shih Tsu (Kublai)	1260 A.D.	Died 1294 A.D. Grandson of Gengis.
(2)	Ch'êng Tsung (Tämur)	1294 A.D.	Grandson of Kublai. Died 1307 A.D.
(3)	Wu Tsung (Haisan)	1307 A.D.	Great grandson of Kublai. Died 1311 A.D.
(4)	Jên Tsung (Ayurparibhadra)	1311 A.D.	Brother of Wu Tsung. Died 1320 A.D.
(5)	Ying Tsung (Suddhipala)	1320 A.D.	Son of Jên Tsung. Died 1323 A.D.
(6)	T'ai Ting Huang Ti (Yäsun Tämur)	1323 A.D.	Grandson of Kublai. Died 1323 A.D.

(Here follows the short reign of a nameless son of T'ai Ting Huang Ti who succeeded his father but was deposed after less than a month).

Emperor	Enthroned	Details.
(7) Wên Tsung (Togh Tämur)	1328 A.D.	Abdicated 1329 A.D.
	1329 A.D.	Died 1332 A.D. Second son of Wu Tsung.
(8) Ming Tsung (Kusala)	1329 A.D.	Died after reigning for six months. Eldest son of Wu Tsung.
(9) Ning Tsung (Irincinbal)	1332 A.D.	Died 1332 A.D. after a reign of two months. Second son of Ming Tsung.
(10) Shun Ti (Togh-an-tämur)	1333 A.D.	Eldest son of Ming Tsung. Fled from Ta-tu in 1368 A.D. Died 1370 A.D.

THE EMPEROR SHIH TSU 1280 A.D. - 1294 A.D.
PERIOD CHIH YÜAN 1264 A.D. - 1294 A.D.

No. 216. Legend. CHIH YÜAN T'UNG PAO (Coinage of the Perfect Yüan)

THE EMPEROR CH'ÊNG TSUNG 1294 A.D. - 1307 A.D.
PERIOD YÜAN CH'ÊN 1295 A.D. - 1297 A.D. (1297)

No. 217. Legend. YÜAN CH'ÊN T'UNG PAO (Coinage of Beginning Virtue)

PERIOD TA TÊ 1297 A.D. - 1307 A.D.

No. 218. Legend TA TÊ T'UNG PAO (Coinage of Great Virtue)

THE EMPEROR WU TSUNG 1307 A.D. - 1311 A.D.
PERIOD CHIH TA 1308 A.D. - 1311 A.D.

No. 219. Legend. CHIH TA YÜAN PAO (Coinage of Extreme Greatness)
Note. The legend is read in a clockwise direction.
No. 220. Legend. CHIH TA T'UNG PAO (Coinage of Extreme Greatness)
Nos. 221-222. Legend TA YÜAN T'UNG PAO (Coinage of the Great Yüan)
No.221. The legend is written in Mongol seal script. This large coin was cast in 1310 A.D. and circulated at a value of ten normal cash. As it weighed eight times the normal cash weight counterfeiting was discouraged. Some rare examples have on the reverse the Chinese numeral ten below the aperture and its Mongol equivalent above.
No.222. The legend is in orthodox Chinese characters.
Note. This small one cash coin is extremely rare.

THE EMPEROR JÊN TSUNG 1311 A.D. - 1320 A.D.
PERIOD HUANG CH'ING 1312 A.D. - 1314 A.D.

No. 223. Legend. HUANG CH'ING T'UNG PAO (Coinage of the Worthy Empire)

PERIOD YEN YU 1314 A.D. - 1320 A.D.

No. 224. Legend. YEN YU YÜAN PAO (Coinage of Lengthening Protection)
No. 225. Legend. YEN YU T'UNG PAO (Coinage of Lengthening Protection)
No. 226. Legend. YEN YU SAN NIEN (Cast in the third year of the period of Lengthening Protection)

Note. It is doubtful if this piece, presumably cast in 1316 A.D. is an official issue. It is of the highest rarity.

THE EMPEROR YING TSUNG 1320 A.D. - 1323 A.D.
PERIOD CHIH CHIH 1321 A.D. - 1323 A.D.

No. 227. Legend. CHIH CHIH YÜAN PAO (Coinage of Great Healing)
No. 228. Legend. CHIH CHIH T'UNG PAO (Coinage of Great Healing)
No. 229. Legend. CHIH CHIH YÜAN NIEN (Cast in the first year of the period of Great Healing)

Note. This piece, presumably cast in 1321 A.D., is rare, and like No. 226 must be considered as probably not an official issue.

THE EMPEROR T'AI TING HUANG TI 1323 A.D. - 1328 A.D.
PERIOD T'AI TING 1324 A.D. - 1328 A.D.

No. 230. Legend. T'AI TING T'UNG PAO (Coinage of Honourable Peace)

PERIOD CHIH HO 1328 A.D.

No. 231. Legend. CHIH HO YÜAN PAO (Coinage of Extensive Harmony)
No. 232. Legend. CHIH HO T'UNG PAO (Coinage of Extensive Harmony)

Note. With so short a period of production both these coins are very rare, the T'ung Pao issue being excessively so as it is not represented in the cabinets of Taiwan Museum. If, as seems likely, the Yüan Pao issue was always the first cast (the character YÜAN having the meaning of first) the rarity of the T'ung Pao issue is explained.

THE EMPEROR WÊN TSUNG 1328 A.D. - 1332 A.D.
PERIOD CHIH SHUN 1330 A.D. - 1332 A.D.

No. 233. Legend. CHIH SHUN YÜAN PAO (Coinage of Perfect Obedience)
No. 234. Legend. CHIH SHUN T'UNG PAO (Coinage of Perfect Obedience)
No. 235. Legend. CHIH SHUN JEN SHEN (Perfect Obedience 1332 A.D.)

Note. Wên Tsung's reign was interrupted when he was deposed in February 1329 A.D. being restored to the throne in September of the same year. The period title, T'ien Li, chosen for his reign was replaced by Chih Shun. This title, Chih Shun was also used by his successor Ning Tsung, who came to the throne at the age of six and after a reign of two months died. However as Ning Tsung is not recorded as having issued any coins there is no difficulty. The legend of No. 235 introduces the use of a Chinese system of dating which is quite common on some coins of the Republic of China, namely the sexagenary cycle. Each year is allocated one of the Ten Celestial Stems, Jen being the ninth. The cycle repeats itself every sixty years and the year during the reign of Wên Tsung when the two characters Jen and Shen coincide is 1332 A.D., the last year of the reign.

THE EMPEROR SHUN TI 1333 A.D. - 1368 A.D.
PERIOD YÜAN T'UNG 1333 A.D - 1335 A.D.

No. 236. Legend. YÜAN T'UNG YÜAN PAO (Coinage of the Beginning of Unity)

Note. The repetition of the character YÜAN in the legend is considered to be improper. This is a rare coin and is probably not an official issue.

No. 237. Legend. YÜAN T'UNG T'UNG PAO (Coinage of the Beginning of Unity)

Note. The characters transliterated by T'UNG differ so there is no improper repetition in the legend.

PERIOD CHIH YÜAN 1335 A.D. - 1341 A.D.

No. 238. Legend. CHIH YÜAN YÜAN PAO (Coinage of Perfect Yüan)

Note. For the second time during this reign the legend of a coin contains an improper repetition. This is also a rare coin and cannot be considered an official issue.

No. 239. Legend. CHIH YÜAN T'UNG PAO (Coinage of Perfect Yüan)

Note. The legend is written in Mongol seal script, the second and last use of the Uigur language on a Chinese coin. It will be remembered that this legend in orthodox Chinese characters was used by Shih Tsu (No. 216).

No. 240. Legend. CHIH YÜAN WU HUO (Flourishing Coinage of Perfect Yüan)

PERIOD CHIH CHÊNG 1341 A.D. - 1368 A.D.

No. 241. Legend. CHIH CHÊNG T'UNG PAO (Coinage of Extreme Verity)

Note. These coins were first issued in 1351 A.D. in four values, one, two, three and ten cash and some coins bear on the reverse their value in Chinese and/or Mongol numbers. Some coins also bear a number in Uigur to indicate the year of issue. (Mao for 1351 A.D., Ssu for 1353 A.D., and Shen for 1356 A.D. are known to exist.)

No. 242. Legend. CHIH CHÊNG (Extreme Verity)

Note. This coin with abbreviated legend belongs to the declining years of the Dynasty.

No. 243. Legend. CHIH CHÊNG CHIH PAO (The Very Coinage of Extreme Verity)

Note. On the reverse appears the character CHI (Happy) and a value in terms of the paper money then flooding the country. It was however too late to stem the flood of support for the Ming faction. The second character Chih (Possessive Case) suggests that counterfeiting was rife.

THE MING DYNASTY 1368 A.D. - 1644 A.D.

With the downfall of the Yüan Dynasty China was once again ruled by a native line of Emperors. It was the last such dynasty in China's history. The founder of the dynasty, T'ai Tsu, was a remarkable man; formerly a Buddhist priest he had left the seclusion of monastic life to join the forces striving against the alien dynasty which then ruled China. His leadership soon brought him to the forefront of the struggle and with the capture of Pekin in 1368 A.D. he was the obvious choice for Emperor. The struggle against the Mongols continued for many years and not until 1382 A.D. were they driven from Yun-Nan, their last foothold on Chinese soil.

The coinage of this dynasty shows two innovations...(a) inferior metal was used in casting the coins and a coating of varnish hid the deficiencies, thus giving a dark, almost black appearance to the coins. Those coins cast from good quality metal have a bright surface. (b) The Emperor Shih Tsung decided in 1527 A.D. to honour those of his ancestors who had either not issued any coins or had issued but a small number by issuing coins bearing their period titles. These supplementary issues can be distinguished from the original issues, where these actually had been made, by their smaller size and lighter weight. There had been cases in the past when an emperor had continued to issue coins bearing his father's period title lest the populace should think lightly of him for his small issue but never before had so many ancestors been so honoured at the same time. Perhaps Shih Tsung was a coin collector and the empty spaces in his cabinets annoyed him. Being in the position to remedy this state of affairs he availed himself of his opportunity. It must be remembered that coin collecting started in China at a very early date and indeed the Usurper Wang Mang at the beginning of the Christian era based issues of coins on mistaken ideas of the types in use in China in the second millenium B.C.

Many of the Emperors of this dynasty issued coins in five different sizes circulating at values of one, two, three, five and ten cash. Their varying sizes differentiate them as this dynasty did not repeat the errors of earlier dynasties in trying to issue a token coinage. Every Emperor with two exceptions used a period title which coincided with the reign. The exceptions are the founder of the dynasty, T'ai Tsu, who used the period title TA CHUNG before the capture of Pekin gave him the Imperial Throne and HUNG WU afterwards, and, the emperor Ying Tsung who used two different period titles, CHÊNG T'UNG AND T'IEN SHUN, to mark the two parts of a reign interrupted for eight years by his deposition.

This dynasty, and in particular the last reign of it, is marked by the large number of rebel war lords who issued copies of the Imperial issues. These they marked on the reverse by a wide variety of private marks, too numerous to be listed and today it is not known which war lord used which mark to signify his issue of coinage. The most attractive of these private issues are those which bear reverse marks of one, two, or even four horses. These private issues are every bit as well made as the official issues and well worth inclusion in the cabinets of the collector.

Contacts between China and the western world multiplied during this dynasty with traders following in the footsteps of the missionaries. In the reign of Shên Tsung that talented man Father Ricci arrived in China earning a high reputation as a mathematician and clockmaker but few converts. The chief points of contact between the twin civilisations of the East and the West are mentioned in the notes to the coins of each reign.

THE EMPERORS OF THE MING DYNASTY 1368 A.D. - 1644 A.D.

Emperor	Enthroned	Details
(1) T'ai Tsu	1368 A.D.	Died 1398 A.D.
(2) Hui Ti	1398 A.D.	Grandson of T'ai Tsu. Died 1402 A.D.
(3) Ch'êng Tsu	1402 A.D.	Son of T'ai Tsu. Died 1424 A.D.
(4) Jên Tsung	1424 A.D.	Son of Ch'êng Tsu. Died 1425 A.D.
(5) Hsüan Tsung	1425 A.D.	Son of Jên Tsung. Died 1435 A.D.
(6) Ying Tsung	1435 A.D.	Son of Hsüan Tsung. Deposed 1449 A.D.
(2nd reign)	1457 A.D.	Died 1464 A.D.
(7) Tai Tsung	1449 A.D.	Brother of Ying Tsung. Deposed

Emperor	Enthroned	Details
		1457 A.D. Died three weeks later.
(8) Hsien Tsung	1464 A.D.	Son of Ying Tsung. Died 1487 A.D.
(9) Hsiao Tsung	1487 A.D.	Son of Hsien Tsung. Died 1505 A.D.
(10) Wu Tsung	1505 A.D.	Son of Hsiao Tsung. Died 1521 A.D.
(11) Shih Tsung	1521 A.D.	Grandson of Hsien Tsung. Died 1567 A.D.
(12) Mu Tsung	1567 A.D.	Son of Shih Tsung. Died 1572 A.D.
(13) Shên Tsung	1572 A.D.	Son of Mu Tsung. Died 1620 A.D.
(14) Kuang Tsung	1620 A.D.	Son of Shên Tsung. Died 1620 A.D.
(15) Hsi Tsung	1620 A.D.	Son of Kuang Tsung. Died 1627 A.D.
(16) Chuang Lieh Ti	1627 A.D.	Brother of Hsi Tsung. Died 1644 A.D.

THE EMPEROR T'AI TSU 1368 A.D. - 1398 A.D.
PERIOD TA CHUNG 1364 A.D. - 1367 A.D.

No. 244. Legend. TA CHUNG T'UNG PAO (Coinage of Great Moderation)

Note. This issue of coins belongs to the time before the dynasty was established in 1368 A.D. Despite the short period of issue they are commonly to be found. They were issued in five denominations... one, two, three, five and ten cash. The following mint names appear on the reverse of the coinage. Che-Kiang, Ho-Nan, Pei-ping in Chih-Li, Shan Tung and Shun Tien Fu.

PERIOD HUNG WU 1368 A.D. - 1398 A.D.

No. 245. Legend. HUNG WU T'UNG PAO (Coinage of Military Reform)
Note. This issue, like the preceding one, was issued in five denominations, one, two, three, five and ten cash. The following mint names appear on the reverse of the coins...Che-Chiang, Ho-Nan, Fu-Chien, Kwei-lin in Kuang-Hsi, Nan-king, Pei-ping in Chih-Li, Shan-Tung and Shun Tien Fu. The increased number of mints is easily understandable.

THE EMPEROR HUI TI 1398 A.D. - 1402 A.D.
PERIOD CHIEN WÊN 1398 A.D. - 1402 A.D.

No. 246. Legend. CHIEN WÊN T'UNG PAO (Coinage of Great Elegance)
Note. These coins were cast in 1527 A.D. by the emperor Shih Tsung when supplementary issues were made to honour his ancestors who had either not issued any coinage or had issued but few coins. These supplementary issues were made in small numbers and are rare. The Emperor Hui Ti was faced by a revolt led by his uncle, the Prince of Yen, and in 1402 A.D. Nan-king fell to the rebels and Hui Ti disappeared. The prince of Yen assumed the empty throne with the title of Ch'êng Tsu.

THE EMPEROR CH'ÊNG TSU 1402 A.D. - 1424 A.D.
PERIOD YUNG LO 1402 A.D. - 1424 A.D.

No. 247. Legend. YUNG LO T'UNG PAO (Coinage of Eternal Joy)
Note. This rare coin was cast in 1527 A.D. by the Emperor Shih Tsung as a supplementary issue, none having been cast by the Emperor Ch'êng Tsu. During this reign the capital was transferred from Nan-king to Pekin.

THE EMPEROR JÊN TSUNG 1424 A.D. - 1425 A.D.
PERIOD HUNG HSI 1424 A.D. - 1425 A.D.

No. 248. Legend. HUNG HSI T'UNG PAO (Coinage of Steady Reform)
Note. The Emperor Jên Tsung did not issue any coins and this piece, a rare one, was one of the supplementary issues made by the Emperor Shih Tsung in 1527 A.D.

THE EMPEROR HSÜAN TSUNG 1425 A.D. - 1435 A.D.
PERIOD HSÜAN TÊ 1425 A.D. - 1435 A.D.

No. 249. Legend. HSÜAN TÊ T'UNG PAO (Coinage of Proclaimed Virtue)
Note. Small numbers of these cash were cast in 1433 A.D. by the mints at Nan-king and Che-Chiang; none however is known to show the mint name on the reverse. In 1527 A.D. the Emperor Shih Tsung issued a supplementary issue of these coins. This second issue, a rare coin, is to be distinguished by its lighter weight.

THE EMPEROR YING TSUNG 1435 A.D. - 1464 A.D.
PERIOD CHÊNG T'UNG 1435 A.D. - 1449 A.D.

No. 250. Legend. CHÊNG T'UNG T'UNG PAO (Coinage of True Unity)
Note. The Chinese characters transliterated T'UNG differ so no improper repetition occurs in the legend. No coins were cast by this Emperor and this rare piece is a supplementary issue made by the Emperor Shih Tsung in 1527 A.D. In 1449 A.D. Ying Tsung lost the throne to Tai Tsung but regained it in 1457 A.D.

SECOND REIGN 1457 A.D. - 1464 A.D.
PERIOD T'IEN SHUN 1457 A.D. - 1464 A.D.

No. 251. Legend. T'IEN SHUN T'UNG PAO (Coinage of Celestial Obedience)
Note. No coins were cast during this period and this rare coin was a supplementary issue made by the Emperor Shih Tsung in 1527 A.D.

THE EMPEROR TAI TSUNG 1449 A.D. - 1457 A.D.
PERIOD CHING T'AI 1449 A.D. - 1457 A.D.

No. 252. Legend. CHING T'AI T'UNG PAO (Coinage of Exalted Prospects)
Note. No coins were issued by this Emperor and this is part of the supplementary issue made by the Emperor Shih Tsung in 1527 A.D. It is a rare coin.

THE EMPEROR HSIEN TSUNG 1464 A.D. - 1487 A.D.
PERIOD CH'ÊNG HUA 1464 A.D. - 1487 A.D.

No. 253. Legend. CH'ÊNG HUA T'UNG PAO (Coinage of Wide Completion)
Note. This Emperor did not issue any coins. This rare piece is part of the supplementary issue made by the Emperor Shih Tsung in 1527 A.D.

THE EMPEROR HSIAO TSUNG 1487 A.D. - 1505 A.D.
PERIOD HUNG CHIH 1487 A.D. - 1505 A.D.

No. 254. Legend. HUNG CHIH T'UNG PAO (Coinage of Healing Lustre)
Note. Hsiao Tsung did not issue any coinage and this rare coin is part of a supplementary issue made by the Emperor Shih Tsung in 1527 A.D.

No. 255. Legend. HUNG CHIH CHIH PAO (The Very Coinage of Healing Lustre)
Note. This legend is not recorded by the older Chinese numi smatic works and must be considered non-official. The second character transliterated CHIH implies possession and is best translated by 'Very' or 'Genuine'.

THE EMPEROR WU TSUNG 1505 A.D. - 1521 A.D.
PERIOD CHÊNG TÊ 1505 A.D. - 1521 A.D.

No. 256. Legend. CHÊNG TÊ T'UNG PAO (Coinage of True Virtue)
Note. The legend of this coin is a favourite for use as an amulet and many of these coins will be found with ornamental rims and reverses decorated with dragons and other designs. During this reign the first European sea-farers reached the coasts of China, Jorge Alvares in 1513 A.D. and Rafael Perestello three years later. In a few years trading posts had been set up along the coastline of Kuang-Tung and Fu-Chien provinces.

THE EMPEROR SHIH TSUNG 1521 A.D. - 1567 A.D.
PERIOD CHIA CHING 1521 A.D. - 1567 A.D.

No. 257. Legend. CHIA CHING T'UNG PAO (Coinage of Increasing Calm)
Note. This Emperor, in order to bring honour to his ancestors, and also to himself, cast and issued small numbers of coins bearing the Period Titles of those of his ancestors who had either issued no coinage during their respective reigns, or had issued but few coins. During this reign the disregard for local laws and customs shown by the Portuguese traders along the South East coasts of China led to the destruction of their trading posts and their expulsion from China. Those traders who survived this process settled at Macao which has remained a centre for Portuguese trading interests ever since.

THE EMPEROR MU TSUNG 1567 A.D. - 1572 A.D.
PERIOD LUNG CH'ING 1567 A.D. - 1572 A.D.

No. 258. Legend. LUNG CH'ING T'UNG PAO (Coinage of Prosperous Benefit)
Note. These coins were first cast in 1570 A.D. Some have a reverse legend...T'AI P'ING T'UNG PAO (Coinage of Great Peace). See Nos. 362 et seq. for coins with this legend issued by the T'ai P'ing rebels in the nineteenth century.

THE EMPEROR SHÊN TSUNG 1572 A.D. - 1620 A.D.
PERIOD WAN LI 1572 A.D. - 1620 A.D.

No. 259. Legend. WAN LI T'UNG PAO (Coinage of the Myriad Succession)
Note. On the reverse of some coins will be found the mint name of the Board of Works Mint in the capital, Pekin, and on others a horse appears above or below the aperture. One remarkable coin has on the reverse the mint name of Che-Chiang in Manchu. This must have

been issued by the Manchu armies during their invasion of China. During this long reign both Spain and Russia attempted to establish diplomatic relations with the Imperial Court but without success as the Chinese regarded every other nation as either a vassal state of China or else as barbarians unworthy of notice. In 1580 A.D. Matteo Ricci, an Italian Jesuit priest arrived in Macao and after several years managed to obtain permission to live in Pekin. He died there in 1610 A.D. without any success in establishing a native church, but his diligent studies of the Chinese language paved the way for those who were to follow him.

THE EMPEROR KUANG TSUNG 1620 A.D.
PERIOD T'AI CH'ANG 1620 A.D.

No. 260. Legend. T'AI CH'ANG T'UNG PAO (Coinage of Honourable Prosperity)
Note. The Emperor Kuang Tsung reigned for only thirty days and since his issue of coinage was but small his son Hsi Tsung, who succeeded his father on the throne at the age of fifteen, caused a further issue to be made lest the common people should think lightly of an emperor who had issued so few coins.

No. 261. Legend. T'AI CH'ANG T'IEN CH'I. (Honourable Prosperity, Celestial Beginning)
Note. This piece, in the Schjöth Collection in Oslo, bears the Period Titles of this and the following reign. It is not a coin and perhaps it was made to commemorate the supplementary issue mentioned in No. 260.

THE EMPEROR HSI TSUNG 1620 A.D. - 1627 A.D.
PERIOD T'IEN CH'I 1620 A.D. - 1627 A.D.

No. 262. Legend. T'IEN CH'I T'UNG PAO (Coinage of Celestial Beginning)
Note. This coin was issued in six denominations...one, two, five, ten, one hundred and one thousand cash. The following mint names appear on the reverse ....Board of Revenue, Board of Works, Che-Chiang, Chen Ting Fu, Ho-Nan, Hsuan Fu Cheng and Yun-Nan. Ch'ên Yu Liang, a rebel leader at the close of the Yüan dynasty, also issued a coin with the legend T'IEN CH'I T'UNG PAO (See No. 344). The two issues of one cash coins may most readily be distinguished by the shape of the character T'IEN. The Ming issue has the two cross strokes much the same size while the rebel issue of the fourteenth century shows the upper cross stroke much shorter than the lower. Since Ch'ên Yu Liang did not issue a denomination higher than one cash there is no problem with the higher denominations. In 1622 A.D. the Dutch made an attack on the Portuguese trading post at Macao and after its failure settled on the Pescadores Islands, between China and Formosa, and a few years later on Formosa itself. They were not driven from Formosa until 1683 A.D.

THE EMPEROR CHUANG LIEH TI 1627 A.D. - 1644 A.D.
PERIOD CH'UNG CHÊNG 1627 A.D. - 1644 A.D.

No. 263. Legend. CH'UNG CHÊNG T'UNG PAO (Coinage of Exalted Dignity)
Note. This Emperor, the last of the Ming Dynasty, probably issued more coins than all his predecessors. Two varieties of obverse

will be found -

(A) The character CHÊNG has straight flanking strokes
(B) The character CHÊNG has diverging flanking strokes.

There seems to be no explanation for this; both are equally common and all mints seem to have issued both varieties.

The following mint names are to be found on the reverse of the coins .. Board of Revenue, Board of Works, Chia-ting in Ssu-Ch'uan, Ching-chao in Shan-Tung, Chung-chao in Ssu-Ch'uan, Chung-ching in Ssu-Ch'uan, Hsuan Fu Cheng in An-Hui, Kung-cheng in Chih-Li, Kwang-chao in Kuang-Tung, Kwei-chao, Lu-chao in Ssu-Ch'uan, Nan-king, Tai-ping in Chiang-Su and Yu-lin in Shen-Hsi. The preponderance of southern mint towns is noticeable and understandable. One rare coin has on the reverse the mint name of Chiang-Su in Manchu, probably issued by the invading Manchu armies. Many War Lord issues will be found of this reign, marked on the reverse with varying numbers of horses etc. Yet other coins will be found with the date in cyclical characters on the reverse, again probably War Lord issues.

No. 264. Legend. CH'UNG CHENG NIEN TSAO (Cast in the time of Exalted Dignity)

Note. This is probably not an official issue.

In 1644 A.D. Chuang Lieh Ti hanged himself in despair when the rebel Li-Tzu-cheng seized the capital and declared himself emperor. During his reign the first British traders sailed into Canton but pre-occupied as Britain was with India for the next century trade grew but slowly.

THE CH'ING DYNASTY 1616 A.D. - 1911 A.D.

While the Ch'ing Dynasty is usually regarded as commencing in 1644 A.D. when the capital Pekin fell to the invading Manchu armies and Chuang Lieh Ti, the last of the Ming emperors committed suicide, partly from despair and partly in anguish at the treachery of his general, Li Tzu Cheng (See No. 354), it is more convenient from a numismatic point of view to commence with Nurhachu, the fifth in the line of tribal leaders and the first to issue coins. His coinage had the legend written in Manchu, though he also issued coins with Chinese legends.

During the course of this dynasty the population of China increased rapidly and with this went an increase in trade with the West. Both factors caused a demand for an ample supply of coinage and a large number of mints was set up to meet the demand. The following list of mints and the date at which each became operational during the Ch'ing Dynasty will also indicate the rapid nature of the Manchu conquest of China. Chang-chau in Fu-Chien (1680), Che-Chiang (1649), Ching-chao in Hu-Pei (1646), Fu-Chien (1649), Ho-Nan (1647), Hsiang-yang in Hu-Pei (1650-1653), Hsuan Fu in Chih-Li (1645), Hu-Nan (1667), Kwei-lin in Kuang-Hsi (1667), Lin-ching in Shan-Tung (1644), Ning-po in Che-Chiang (1649), Shan-Tung (1649), Su-chau in Chiang-Su (1667), Taiwan (1689), Ta-tung in Shan-Hsi (1645), Tai-yüen in Shan-Hsi (1645), Wu-chang in Hu-Pei (1650), Yang-ho in Shan-Hsi (1649), Yen-shui in Shen-Hsi (1644)

Two points may be noted in this list. (a) The mint at Hsiang-yang was open for the short period of only three years, hence the coins bearing this mint name are very uncommon. (b) Taiwan, maybe better known as Formosa, was the last part of China to be held by Ming adherents and was not conquered by Manchu forces until 1683.

The following list of Emperors of this Dynasty will be of interest -

Emperor	Enthroned	Details
T'ai Tsu (Nurhachu)	1616 *	Died 1626 A.D.
T'ai Tsung	1626 *	Son of T'ai Tsu. Died 1643 A.D.
Shih Tsu	1643 A.D.	Son of T'ai Tsung. Died 1661 A.D.
Shêng Tsu	1661 A.D.	Son of Shih Tsu. Died 1722 A.D.
Shih Tsung	1722 A.D.	Son of Shêng Tsu. Died 1735 A.D.
Kao Tsung	1735 A.D.	Son of Shih Tsung. Abdicated 1796 A.D. Died 1799 aged 88 years.
Jên Tsung	1796 A.D.	15th son of Kao Tsung. Died 1820 A.D.
Hsüan Tsung	1820 A.D.	Son of Jên Tsung. Died 1850 A.D.
Wên Tsung	1850 A.D.	Son of Hsüan Tsung. Died 1861 A.D.
Mu Tsung	1861 A.D.	Son of Wên Tsung. Died 1875 A.D.
Tê Tsung	1875 A.D.	Grandson of Hsüan Tsung. Died 1908 A.D. (Emperor aged 4, murdered 1908 A.D.)

(Tzu Hsi - the Dowager Empress - ruled as Regent from 1875 A.D. to 1889 A.D. and from 1898 A.D. to 1908 A.D. Finding herself dying she had the Emperor murdered.)

Pu I	1908 A.D.	Nephew of Tê Tsung. Emperor at the age of two. Abdicated 1912 A.D.

NOTE. The two rulers marked * were Manchu chieftains and were not Emperors of China.

As regards the coinage the only innovation was the production of milled coins during the last years of the nineteenth century. These, not being cash, are excluded from this book. As to be expected Manchu mint names appear on the reverse of most of the coinage, but otherwise the cash coinage of China followed the pattern set so many centuries earlier until its close.

THE CH'ING DYNASTY 1616 A.D. - 1911 A.D.
THE EMPEROR T'AI TSU KAO 1616 A.D. - 1626 A.D.
PERIOD T'IEN MING 1616 A.D. - 1626 A.D.

No. 265. Legend. ABKAI FULINGGA HAN JIHA (Imperial Coinage of Heavenly Mandate)
Note. The legend of this coin is written in Manchu and is read - left, right, top, bottom.

No.266. Legend. T'IEN MING T'UNG PAO (Coinage of the Heavenly Mandate)
Note. Nurhachu was a Manchu chieftain and while he never was enthroned as Emperor of China he was given the posthumous titles and honours of an emperor. During his lifetime the Manchus drove the Chinese forces from Mukden and conquered parts of Korea and Mongolia. The use of Chinese legends shows perhaps the course he meant the Manchus to follow.

THE EMPEROR T'AI TSUNG 1626 A.D. - 1643 A.D.
PERIOD T'IEN TSUNG (Celestial Understanding) 1627 A.D.-1635 A.D.

No. 267. Legend. SURA NI HAN JIHA (Coinage of Celestial Understanding)
Note. The legend is written in Manchu and is read - left, bottom, top and right. T'ai Tsung was in reality a Manchu chieftain to whom after his death the titles and honours due to an Emperor were given. In 1636

A.D. T'ai Tsung adopted the title Ch'ing (Pure) as the name of the dynasty and so it is rather surprising that he did not issue any coinage with Chinese legends. In the same year he adopted Ch'ing Tê as a period title but though it continued as such until his death no coinage was issued using this period title in the legend. This is the second of the only two Chinese coins with Manchu legends and both are rather rare.

THE EMPEROR SHIH TSU 1643 A.D. - 1661 A.D.
PERIOD SHUN CHIH 1643 A.D. - 1661 A.D.

No. 268. Legend SHUN CHIH T'UNG PAO (Coinage of Obedient Rule)
Note. There are five different types of reverse found with this issue.
(A) Reverse blank or with character Yi for one cash. These coins were cast during the years 1644 A.D. - 1648 A.D.
(B) Reverse with BOO (Manchu form of PAO) to left of aperture and either Board of Revenue or Board of Works in Manchu to the right. These coins were issued in the first year of the reign, 1644 A.D., but despite their short period of issue are not particularly scarce.
(C) Coins issued between the years 1644 A.D. and 1649 A.D. bearing on the reverse one of the following mint names in Chinese... Board of Revenue, Board of Works, Che-Chiang, Chi-chao in Chih-Li, Ching-chao in Hu-Pei, Fu-Chien, Ho-Nan, Hsiang-yang in Hu-Pei, Hsüan Fu in Chih-Li, Lin-ching in Shan-Tung, Mi-yun in Chih-Li, Ning-po in Che-Chiang, Shan-Hsi, Shan-Tung, Ta-tung in Shan-Hsi, Tai-ping in Kuang-Hsi, Tai- yuan in Shan-Hsi, Wu-chang in Hu-Pei and Yang-ho in Shan-Hsi.
(D) Coins issued betwenn 1650 A.D. and 1661 A.D. with YI LI (One Cash) to the left of the aperture and one of the following mint names in Chinese to the right ....Board of Revenue, Board of Works, Che-Chiang, Chi-chao in Chih-Li, Fu-Chien, Ho-Nan, Hsüan Fu in Chih-Li, Lin-ching in Shan-Tung, Mi-yun in Chih-Li, Nan-King, Ning-po in Che-Chiang, Shan-Tung, Shen-Hsi, Tai-yuan in Shan-Hsi, Wu-chang in Hu-Pei and Yang-ho in Shan-Hsi.
(E) Coins issued betwenn 1650 A.D. and 1661 A.D. bearing on the reverse the mint name in both Chinese and Manchu of one of the following mints.....Che-Chiang, Chi-chao in Chih-Li, Ho-Nan, Hsüan Fu in Chih-Li, Lin-ching in Shan-Tung, Nan-king, Ning-po in Che-Chiang, Shan-Tung, Shen-Hsi, Ta-tung in Shan-Hsi, Tai-yuan in Shan-Hsi and Wu-chang in Hu-Pei

THE EMPEROR SHÊNG TSU 1661 A.D. - 1722 A.D.
PERIOD K'ANG HSI 1661 A.D. - 1722 A.D.

No. 269. Legend. K'ANG HSI T'UNG PAO (Coinage of Steady Prosperity)
Note. Two types of reverse are to be found with this coinage.
(A) Coins issued between 1661 A.D. and 1667 A.D. with BOO (PAO in Manchu) to the left of the aperture and one of three mint names in Manchu to the right....Board of Revenue, Board of Works, Kwei-lin in Kuang-Hsi.
(B) Coins issued between 1667 A.D. and 1722 A.D. bearing one of the following mint names in both Manchu and Chinese...Chang-chau in Fu-chien, Che-Chiang, Chi-chao in Chih-Li, Fu-Chien, Ho-Nan, Hsüan Fu in Chih-Li, Hu-Nan, Kuang-Tung, Kwei-

lin in Kuang-Hsi, Lin-ching in Shan-Tung, Nan-king, Ning-po in Che-Chiang, Shan-Tung, Shen-Hsi, Su-chao in Chiang-Su, Ta-tung in Shan-Hsi, Taiwan (Formosa), Tai-yuan in Shan-Hsi, Wu-chang in Hu-Pei and Yun-Nan.

The twenty Chinese characters found on the reverse of this type form a poem according to the rules of Chinese poetry and the collecting of them was a favourite target for Chinese collectors. With a period of issue exceeding fifty years most are very commonly to be found but some, particularly Taiwan, are rather scarce.

No. 270. Legend K'ANG HSI T'UNG PAO (Coinage of Steady Prosperity) This coin is an interesting obverse variety of the preceding number. The left hand vertical stroke of the character HSI is missing. These are called Lohan Cash, the Lohans being disciples of Buddha, and being cast, so it is said, from the metal obtained from the idols from Buddhist temples, are believed to contain gold. I once had the opportunity of measuring the specific gravity of a dozen specimens and not one deviated in the least from the figure found by measuring the specific gravity of normal K'ANG HSI cash so their gold content is a myth. They bear on the reverse the mint name of the Board of Revenue and in very rare cases that of Che-Chiang.

THE EMPEROR SHIH TSUNG 1722 A.D. - 1735 A.D.
PERIOD YUNG CHÊNG 1723 A.D. - 1735 A.D.

No. 271. Legend. YUNG CHÊNG T'UNG PAO (Coinage of Stable Peace) Note. In this reign the reverse of the coinage settled into the normal Ch'ing type, i.e. the character BOO (PAO in Manchu) to the left of the aperture and the mint name in Manchu to the right. The following mint names will be found....Board of Revenue, Board of Works, Chang-chau in Fu-Chien, Che-Chiang, Chi-nan in Shan-Tung, Fu-Chien, Ho-Nan, Hu-Nan, Kuang-Tung, Kwei-chao, Kung-chang in Kan-Su, Nan-chang in Chiang-Hsi, Ngan-Hwei (Anhui), Shan-Hsi, Su-chao in Chiang-Su, Ssu-Ch'uan, Wu-chang in Hu-Pei and Yun-Nan.

THE EMPEROR KAO TSUNG 1735 A.D. - 1796 A.D.
PERIOD CH'IEN LUNG 1735 A.D. - 1796 A.D.

No. 272. Legend CH'IEN LUNG T'UNG PAO (Coinage of Celestial Benefit)

Note. Three types of reverses are to be found in this issue.

(A) Reverse blank. It must be assumed that these coins were cast in the initial year of the reign, 1735 A.D.

(B) The Chinese characters YI LI (One cash) to the left of the aperture and the mint name of Kwei-chao in Manchu to the right. This is a rare piece and it is difficult to understand the reappearance of a reverse type discarded seventy years previously.

(C) The Manchu BOO (translation of Chinese PAO) to the left of the aperture and one of the following mint names in Manchu to the right....Board of Revenue, Board of Works, Che-Chiang, Chih-Li, Chi-nan in Shan-Tung, Fu-Chien, (Two different marks), Hu-Nan, Ili, Chiang-Su, Kuang-Tung, Kwei-chao, Kwei-lin in Kuang-Hsi, Nan-Chang in Chiang-Hsi, Shan-Hsi, Shen-Hsi, Ssu-Ch'uan, Taiwan, Wu-chang in Hu-Pei and Yun-Nan.
The Taiwan mint, probably issuing but few coins, is the rarest. This reign was marked by great unrest caused by poverty, as

the population of China exploded from sixty million to over three hundred million and for some time effective control was lost over large areas of Shan-Tung, Ho-Nan and the Island of Taiwan. In 1792 A.D. Lord Macartney led a mission to Pekin seeking to have other ports than Canton opened to British ships. His failure is perhaps to be attributed to the fact that not a single British subject could be found to act as interpreter. Kao Tsung is probably today best remembered as an art connoisseur, forming the world famous Palace Collection of painting, calligraphy, porcelain and bronzes. He ordered the collection of all books in Chinese and had nearly eighty thousand volumes copied and complete libraries of them established in Pekin, Mukden and five other provincial capitals. Outliving fourteen of his sons he abdicated in 1796 A.D. in favour of his fifteenth son Jên Tsung and died three years later at the age of eighty eight, the oldest Emperor of China.

THE EMPEROR JÊN TSUNG 1796 A.D. - 1820 A.D.
PERIOD CHIA CH'ING 1796 A.D. - 1820 A.D.

No. 273. Legend CHIA CH'ING T'UNG PAO (Coinage of Increasing Good)

Note. The reverse of this issue bears to the left of the aperture BOO (Manchu for PAO) and one of the following mint names in Manchu to the right....Board of Revenue, Board of Works, Che-Chiang, Chih-Li, Fu-Chien, (both marks), Hu-Nan, Ili, Chiang-Su, Kuang-Tung, Kwei-chao, Kwei-lin in Kuang-Hsi, Nan-chang in Chiang-Hsi, Ngan-Hwei (Anhui), Shan-Hsi, Shan-Tung, Shen-Hsi, Ssu-Ch'uan, Ta-tung in Shan-Hsi, Wu-chang in Hu-Pei and Yun-Nan.
Iron cash were cast at the Board of Revenue Mint at Pekin, the first time this metal had been used for the coinage since the times of the Sung Dynasty.

THE EMPEROR HSÜAN TSUNG 1820 A.D. - 1850 A.D.
PERIOD TAO KUANG 1821 A.D. - 1850 A.D.

No. 274. Legend. TAO KUANG T'UNG PAO (Coinage of Brilliant Reason)

Note. Two types of reverse will be found on the coins of this issue.

(A) BOO (Manchu for PAO) to the left of the aperture and one of three mint names in Chinese to the right...Ning-po, Shen-Hsi and Su-chao. It is difficult to explain the reappearance of mint names in Chinese after a century's disuse.

(B) BOO (Manchu for Pao) to the left of the aperture and one of the following mint names in Manchu to the right....Board of Revenue, Board of Works, Che-Chiang, Chih-Li, Fu-Chien, (Both marks), Hu-Nan, Ili, Chiang-Su, Kuang-Tung, Kwei-chao, Kwei-lin in Kuang-Hsi, Nan-chang in Chiang-Hsi, Shan-Hsi, Shan-Tung, Shen -Hsi, Ssu-Ch'uan, Ta-tung in Shan-Hsi, Wu-chang in Hu-Pei and Yun-Nan.

During this reign occurred the Opium War 1839 A.D. - 1842 A.D. between Britain and China. The H.E.I.C. found opium their most profitable export to China but disregarding the physical evils caused by the drug the Chinese government was disturbed to see so many million dollars of silver leaving the country each year to pay for what was both a luxury and an evil. There was a dearth of silver for bullion and the copper cash became progressively smaller and smaller. The defeat of the Manchu soldiers by the better discipline and firepower of the British and sepoy troops lessened the fear the Chinese held for these troops and led to the Tai P'ing rebellion and eventually to the end of the Manchu Dynasty and the establishment of the Republic of China. The immediate results of the war was the opening of the ports of Amoy, Foochow, Ning-po and Shanghai to British traders as well as Canton. Two years later the privilege of trading through these ports was extended to American merchants and the long involvement of the U.S.A. with Far Eastern affairs began. The mint at Nan-chang in Chiang-Hsi issued some iron coins during this period, the result perhaps of the shortage of copper for coinage.

THE EMPEROR WÊN TSUNG 1850 A.D. - 1861 A.D.
PERIOD HSIEN FÊNG 1851 A.D. - 1861 A.D.

No. 275. Legend. HSIEN FÊNG T'UNG PAO (Coinage of Great Abundance)

Note. The reverse of this issue has BOO (Manchu for PAO) to the left of the aperture and one of the following mint names in Manchu to the right....Board of Revenue, Board of Works, Che-Chiang, Chih-Li, Chi-Nan in Shan-Tung, Fu-Chien (both mint marks), Hu-Nan, Ili, Chiang-Su, Kuang-Tung, Kwei-chao, Kwei-lin in Kuang-Hsi, Kung-chang in Kan-Su, Nan-chang in Chiang-Hsi, Shan-Hsi, Shan-Tung, Shen-Hsi, Ssu-Ch'uan, Wu-chang in Hu-Pei and Yun-Nan.
Iron coins were issued by the following mints...Board of Revenue, Chih-Li, Fu-Chien, and Chiang-Su. This was the last reign in which iron was used for coinage.
During this reign the T'ai P'ing rebellion caused chaos in China and the Treasury was forced to issue token or so-called heavy coinage. Those issued using the T'UNG PAO legend ending were as follows...
Five cash coins from the Board of Revenue Mint.
Ten cash coins from the mints of the Board of Works and Fu-Chien.

No. 276. Legend. HSIEN FÊNG YÜAN PAO (Coinage of Great Abundance)

Note. This issue of ' Heavy ' coinage was the first to use the YÜAN PAO type of legend for over five hundred years. The issue was as follows.... One hundred cash coins were issued by the following mints ....Board of Revenue, Board of Works, Chih-Li, Chi-nan in Shan-Tung, Fu-Chien, Ho-Nan, Chiang-Su, Shen-Hsi, and Wu-chang in Hu-Pei.
In addition to these the Board of Revenue Mint issued coins with the value of two hundred, five hundred cash and one thousand cash. The Board of Works Mint issued coins with a value of five hundred and one thousand cash.

No. 277. Legend. HSIEN FÊNG CHUNG PAO (Heavy Coinage of Great Abundance)

Note. Five cash coins were issued by the following mints...Board of Works, Chang-te in Hu-Nan, Chih-Li, Hu-Nan and Kung-chang in Chiang-Su. Iron coins of this value were issued by Chih-Li and Hu-Nan Mints.
Ten cash coins were issued by the following mints...Board of Revenue, Board of Works, Chang-te in Hu-Nan, Che-Chiang, Chih-Li, Chi-chao in Chih-Li, Hu-Nan, Hu-Pei, Chiang-Hsi, Chiang-Su, Kuang-Hsi, Kwei-chao, Kwei-lin in Kuang-Hsi, Kung-chang in Kan-

Su, Nan-chang in Chiang-Hsi, Shan-Hsi, Shan-Tung, Ssu-Ch'uan, Taiwan, Wu-chang in Hu-Pei and Yun-Nan. Iron coins of this value were issued by the Board of Revenue Mint.
Twenty cash coins were cast at the mints of Fu-Chien and Wu-chang in Hu-Pei. The latter mint also issued thirty cash coins.
Fifty cash coins came from the following mints...Board of Revenue, Board of Works, Chih-Li, Fu-Chien, Ho-Nan, Hu-Nan, Kung-chang in Kan-Su, Nan-chang in Chiang-Hsi, Chiang-Su and Wu-chang in Hu-Pei. During this reign was fought the second war between China and the Western nations. The outcome was the opening of a further ten ports to the shipping of European and American powers and the granting of the right of Christian missionaries to travel and preach where they wished anywhere in China. Another result which is less well known was the introduction of the Pekinese dog to the West.

THE EMPEROR MU TSUNG 1861 A.D. - 1875 A.D.
PERIOD CH'I HSIANG 1861 A.D.

No. 278. Legend. CH'I HSIANG CHUNG PAO (Heavy Coinage of Predestined Happiness)
Note. The period title, Ch'i Hsiang, was the original choice for this reign and was changed to Tung Chih after the palace coup of 1862 A.D. Ten cash coins bearing the CH'I HSIANG legend were cast by the two mints of the capital, the Board of Revenue and the Board of Works, but they must never have been issued in any quantity as they are most uncommon.

PERIOD TUNG CHIH 1862 A.D. - 1875 A.D.

No. 279. Legend. TUNG CHIH T'UNG PAO (Coinage of United Law and Order)
Note. The reverse of the coinage of this issue has BOO (Manchu for PAO) to the left of the aperture and the mint name of one of the following in Manchu to the right....Board of Works, Che-Chiang, Hu-Nan, Chiang-Su, Kuang-Tung, Kwei-lin in Kuang-Hsi, Nan-chang in Chiang-Hsi, Ssu-Ch'uan and Yun-Nan.
During this reign the one cash coins were cast in ever decreasing diameter and the smaller ones are known as ' Depreciated Cash '. They measure as little as eighteen mms in diameter.

No. 280. Legend. TUNG CHIH CHUNG PAO (Heavy Coinage of United Law and Order)
Note. Token or so-called ' Heavy ' coins were issued with a value of ten cash from the following mints....Board of Revenue, Board of Works, Kuang-Tung and Kung-chang in Kan-su.

THE EMPEROR TÊ TSUNG 1875 A.D. - 1908 A.D.
PERIOD KUANG HSÜ 1875 A.D. - 1908 A.D.

No. 281. Legend, KUANG HSÜ T'UNG PAO (Coinage of the Succession of Glory)
Note. The reverse of this issue bears the Manchu equivalent of PAO, BOO, to the left of the aperture and one of the following mint names in Manchu to the right...Board of Revenue, Board of Works, Che-Chiang, Chih-Li, Chi-chao in Chih-Li, Fu-Chien (both mint marks), Ho-Nan, Hu-Nan, Chiang-Su, Kwei-lin in Kuang-Hsi, Kung-chang in Kan-Su, Ta-tung in Shan-Hsi, Wu-chang in Hu-Pei and Yun-Nan.
There exists a silver cash bearing the mint name of the Board of Revenue, the only silver cash I have ever heard of. Perhaps it is a

trial piece or perhaps a presentation coin.

No. 282. Legend. KUANG HSÜ CHUNG PAO (Heavy Coinage of the Succession of Glory)

Note. The aftermaths of the T'ai P'ing disturbances brought about a further issue of token or so-called ' Heavy ' coins. Ten cash coins were cast by the following mints ....Board of Revenue, Board of Works, Hu-Nan and Ta-tung in Shan-Hsi.

During this reign European minting machinery was introduced into China, Kuang-Tung Mint being the first equipped, and two types of milled cash were produced.

(A) A coin bearing the mint name of Kuang-Tung in both Chinese and Manchu. This is probably the first copper milled coin used in China.

(B) Coins bearing the usual BOO and mint name in Manchu came from three mints...Kuang-Tung, Ning-po and Wu-chang. Some of the second type of milled cash have a round aperture, the first time this had appeared on an official issue since the times of the independent states before the Ch'in Dynasty of 255 B.C. - 207 B.C.

The Emperor Tê Tsung succeeded to the throne at the age of four years and during his minority power rested in the hands of the Dowager Empress Tzu Hsi, an ambitious and thoroughly evil woman. Conservative to a degree she failed to see the path that China must follow to keep up with Western technology and when the Emperor reached the age of rule without her took the first opportunity to imprison him in the palace and rule in person. His crime had been to appoint as his advisers men with European education and liberal views. By her actions she doomed the Dynasty to extinction whereas Tê Tsung, who seemed to be thinking along the lines of a constitutional monarchy could probably have saved it. The poorly equipped Chinese forces fell an easy prey to the Japanese who had copied Western tactics and weapons and in 1895 A.D. Taiwan (Formosa) fell to them. The Dowager Empress encouraged the activities of the Boxers (Society of the Fist) and when their murders of missionaries and traders culminated in the siege of the Legations in Pekin in 1900 A.D. troops from Britain, the United States, France, Russia, Austria, Italy, Germany and Japan soon effected their release. The Treaty of Pekin in 1901 A.D. which ended this ' war' forced China to pay reparations of sixty million pound in silver, leading to further inflation, popular discontent and eventually to the Republic of China. In 1908 A.D. the Dowager Empress found herself on the point of death and her last action was somehow characteristic of this formidable woman; she had the Emperor murdered so that he would not survive her and put his reforms into being. The throne devolved to Pu I, a child of two years.

THE EMPEROR PU I 1908 A.D. - 1912 A.D.
PERIOD HSÜAN T'UNG 1909 A.D. - 1912 A.D.

No. 283. Legend. HSÜAN T'UNG T'UNG PAO (Coinage of Proclaimed Unity)

Note. The Chinese characters transliterated T'UNG differ so no improper repetition occurs in the legend.
The reverse shows BOO (Manchu for PAO) to the left of the aperture and the mint name of either the Board of Revenue or Yun-Nan to the right. Milled cash of this type, but with a round aperture, were produced by the Kuang-Tung mint.
Pu I, caught up in the culmination of fifty years unrest and the private ambitions of Yüan Shih Kai abdicated on the 12th February 1912 and the long series of Chinese Imperial cash came to an end after two thousand

years. Pu I made a brief return to ' power ' during the second World War when the Japanese made him their puppet emperor of Manchuria and then the two hundred and twelfth and last Emperor of China faded into obscurity.

CHINESE TURKISTAN

Turkistan, known to the Chinese as Sin-Kiang, the New Province, and to the ancients as Transoxiana, is inhabited by a mixture of nationalities whose rivalry and internal dissensions have led to their conquest by Russia in the West and China in the East. This conquest by China began in the first century A.D. and extended to Kashgar. By the fifth century the Chinese were in retreat and only a stubborn resistance in Loh-nor, a track of marshland six hundred miles east of Kashgar saved China itself from an invasion by the Huns. In 1758 A.D. civil war in Turkistan paved the way for a Chinese invasion and when Dzungaria, a district four hundred miles north of Loh-nor was occupied it is said that more than a million civilians were massacred. Eastern Turkistan was reconquered, each phase being marked by the customary massacre. The Kalmuks and the Khojas, the contending parties in Turkistan, came together and preaching a Holy War loosed hordes of Islamic fanatics on the Chinese troops and hopeful settlers. The Chinese armies suffered extermination on three occasions, in 1825 A.D. in 1830 A.D. and again in 1847 A.D. However without a permanently settled leadership the peoples of Turkistan could only halt the Chinese advance temporarily and despite further risings in 1857 A.D. and in the years between 1864 A.D. and 1872 A.D., the latter led by Yakub Bey, 1877 A.D. saw Chinese rule firmly established. The coins issued by the Chinese for use in Turkistan followed closely the patterns used in the home provinces and the obverse shows the usual legend for the respective reigns. The reverse differs from the usual type in that the mint name is shown in Manchu to the left of the aperture and in Turki to the right. If this is remembered that Turkistan lay six weeks camel caravan time from Pekin it is scarcely surprising that the moulds were locally produced and fall far short of the high standard used in the home provinces. The obverse is very blurred, lacking that clear cut outline of character which had characterised Chinese coins since the T'ang Dynasty, and it is often impossible to read the Turki mint name at all. However the Manchu mint names are usually clear enough to enable the mint to be determined without difficulty.

THE COINS OF TURKISTAN (SINKIANG)

Obverse.	Aksu	Ushi	Yarkand.	Kuchar.
272	1 cash, ten cash.	1 cash	1 cash	
273	1 cash			
274	1, 5 and ten cash.			
275	1, 5, 10, 50 & 100 cash.		10, 50, 100 cash	10 cash
276	100 cash			
277	10 and 50 cash			
279	10 cash		10 cash	10 cash
281	10 cash			10 cash

Note. I feel that this table represents only a portion of the coinage issued in Turkistan but I have listed only those values and mints I have met with. Perhaps in the future it will be extended when fuller information is gathered. The coins of these mints are very much rarer than the usual home province mints and Aksu is the mint name most often found by the collector. Ushi is without question by far the rarest.

DYNASTIES NOT BELONGING TO THE REGULAR LINE.

Cheng Dynasty 304 A.D. - 346 A.D.
Former Liang Dynasty 314 A.D. - 363 A.D.
Later Chao Dynasty 329 A.D. - 351 A.D.
Northern Liang Dynasty 397 A.D. - 439 A.D.
Shu Dynasty 907 A.D. - 925 A.D.
Southern Han Dynasty 917 A.D. - 971 A.D.
Min Dynasty 932 A.D. - 946 A.D.
Later Shu Dynasty 934 A.D. - 965 A.D.
Southern T'ang Dynasty 937 A.D. - 976 A.D.
Hsia Dynasty 982 A.D. - 1227 A.D.
Liao Dynasty 907 A.D. - 1125 A.D.
Chin Dynasty 1115 A.D. - 1234 A.D.

THE CHENG DYNASTY 304 A.D. - 346 A.D.

This short lived Tartar dynasty occupied a portion of North Ssu-Ch'uan. When Li Shou became Emperor in 338 A.D. he was given the title of Chao Wên and marked the change of dynastic name from Cheng to Han by an issue of coins.

THE EMPEROR CHAO WÊN 338 A.D. - 343 A.D.

No. 284. Legend. HAN HSING (Rising Han)

THE FORMER LIANG DYNASTY 314 A.D. - 363 A.D.

When the Chin Emperor Huai Ti died at the hands of the Huns in 313 A.D. Chang Shih, the Governor of Kansu, declared his independence and founded this dynasty. The lands occupied by them were mostly in the western parts of Shen-Hsi and differed from most other short lived dynasties in that they were a prosperous region and so the dynasty was a stable one. Chang Shih assumed the title of Emperor in 315 A.D. and a year earlier issued the only coin attributable to this dynasty. It is interesting to note that even though he had not assumed the imperial titles his name was still regarded as too sacred to appear on the coinage. This is an extremely rare coin, there not being a specimen in the Historical Museum in Taiwan.

THE EMPEROR CHANG SHIH 315 A.D. - 320 A.D.

No. 285. Legend. LIANG TSAO HSIN CH'ÜAN (New Coin of Tsao of Liang)

THE LATER CHAO DYNASTY 329 A.D. - 351 A.D.

Shih Lo, a slave in China, escaped from his bondage and joined himself to a group of Tartar and Hun tribesmen who did not belong to the recognised tribes. His ability as a leader of men soon brought him promotion until he led the confederation in raids on South China, one in 310 A.D. ending with the massacre of 100,000 Chinese civilians. Not having any ambitions to be Emperor, or more likely knowing too well the instability of his hold over men who only followed his standard for the loot it brought them, he withdrew to his base in North Chih-Li and did not assume the title of Emperor until 329 A.D. A successful leader of raiders he may have been but he lacked completely any ability to organise and rule his lands and the dynasty did not long survive his death, no fewer than seven others being emperor in the remaining eighteen years.

THE EMPEROR KAO TSU 329 A.D. - 333 A.D.

No. 286. Legend. FÊNG HUO (Coinage of Abundance)
Note. Shih Lo assumed the title of Kao Tsu but his lowly birth was still remembered against him and none of the later Tartar dynasties claimed descent from his.

THE NORTHERN LIANG DYNASTY 397 A.D. - 439 A.D.

This Tartar dynasty was composed of a group of families which had overrun part of the territory of the Later Liang dynasty in Eastern Kan-Su. Three Emperors ruled over it, Wu Hsüan Wang, the only one to issue coins, ruling for thirty two years. They were finally destroyed by the Mongolian Juan-juan tribesmen in 439 A.D. although a younger son of Wu Hsüan Wang continued to rule a small portion of the area until 441 A.D.

THE EMPEROR WU HSÜAN WANG 401 A.D. - 433 A.D.
PERIOD YUNG AN 401 A.D. - 412 A.D.

No. 287. Legend. YUNG AN I PAI (One Hundred Cash of Eternal Peace)
No. 288. Legend. YUNG AN I CH'IEN (One Hundred Cash of Eternal Peace)

THE SHU DYNASTY 907 A.D. - 925 A.D.

This short lived dynasty was ruled by two Emperors, Wang Chien, who took the title of Kao Tsu, and his son Wang Tsung Yen who was deposed in 925 A.D.

THE EMPEROR KAO TSU 907 A.D. - 918 A.D.
PERIOD YUNG P'ING 911 A.D. - 916 A.D.

No. 289. Legend. YUNG P'ING YÜAN PAO (Coinage of Endless Peace)
Note. The characters of the legend are read in a clockwise direction.

PERIOD T'UNG CHÊNG 916 A.D. - 917 A.D.

No. 290. Legend. T'UNG CHÊNG YÜAN PAO (Coinage of True Unity)
Note. The characters of the legend are read in a clockwise direction.

PERIOD T'IEN HAN 917 A.D. - 918 A.D.

No. 291. Legend. T'IEN HAN YÜAN PAO (Coinage of Celestial Han)
Note. In 917 A.D. the dynastic title was altered to han, hence this legend which is read in a clockwise direction.

PERIOD KUANG T'IEN 917 A.D.

No. 292. Legend. KUANG T'IEN YÜAN PAO (Coinage of Celestial Light)
Note. The characters of the legend are read in a clockwise direction.
No. 293. Legend. TA SHU T'UNG PAO (Coinage of the Great Shu)
Note. In 918 A.D. the dynastic title reverted to Shu, hence this legend.

THE EMPEROR WANG TSUNG YEN 918 A.D. - 925 A.D.
PERIOD CH'IEN TÊ 919 A.D. - 925 A.D.

No. 294. Legend. CH'IEN TÊ YÜAN PAO (Coinage of Celestial Virtue)

PERIOD HSIEN K'ANG 925 A.D.
No. 295. Legend. HSIEN K'ANG YÜAN PAO (Coinage of Great Peace)

Note. The legends of both coins of this Emperor are to be read in a clockwise direction. This Dynasty, of so little importance in the history of China was responsible for a surprisingly large number of coins.

THE SOUTHERN HAN DYNASTY 917 A.D. - 971 A.D.

This Dynasty was founded by Hsiang who first claimed the Imperial title in 905 A.D. and died in either 910 A.D. or 911 A.D. The second ruler was Liu Yen, a younger brother of the founder, and when he took the title of Emperor in 917 A.D. he took the name Kao Tsu. Two of his sons followed him on the throne and the last of the Dynasty was a grandson, Nan Yueh Wang, who fell into the hands of the Sung armies in 971 A.D. dying nine years later.

THE EMPEROR KAO TSU 917 A.D. - 942 A.D.
PERIOD CH'IEN HÊNG 917 A.D. - 925 A.D.

No. 296. Legend. CH'IEN HÊNG T'UNG PAO (Coinage of Pervading Heaven)

No. 297. Legend. CH'IEN HÊNG CHUNG PAO (Heavy Coinage of Pervading Heaven)

PERIOD TA YU 928 A.D. - 942 A.D.

No. 298. Legend. TA YU YÜAN PAO (Coinage of Great Life)

THE MIN DYNASTY 932 A.D. - 946 A.D.

This short lived dynasty ruled over a small area on the eastern littoral of China during the time of the Five Dynasties in North China. It was founded by Wang Yen Chün who assumed the title of Emperor in 932 A.D. and was given the name T'ai Tsung. His father, known as T'ai Tsu, had been governor of the region for more than twenty years and had declared himself independent about the year 907 A.D. without however claiming the imperial titles. After a son, Yen-Han had ruled for less than a year T'ai Tsung became ruler about the year 925 A.D., claiming the title of Emperor seven years later. He died in either 932 A.D. or 934 A.D. and his son K'ang Tsung succeeded him on the throne and ruled some three years. In 938 A.D. Ching Tsung, a brother of T'ai Tsung seized the throne and ruled until his death in 943 A.D. when yet another brother Yen Chĕng ruled until his deposition in 946 A.D. brought the dynasty to a close after fourteen years and four Emperors. Only two of these rulers issued coins, T'ai Tsung and Ching Tsung.

THE EMPEROR T'AI TSUNG 932 A.D. - 932 or 934 A.D.

No. 299. Legend. K'AI YÜAN T'UNG PAO (Coinage of the Inauguration)
Note. This coin was cast in 925 A.D. before T'ai Tsung assumed the title of Emperor. The legend had been used extensively by the T'ang Dynasty but the large size of this issue, diameter 42 mms, makes it readily distinguishable.

THE EMPEROR CHING TSUNG 938 A.D. - 943 A.D.
PERIOD YUNG LUNG 938 A.D. - 942 A.D.

No. 300. Legend. YUNG LUNG YUAN PAO (Coinage of Unceasing Prosperity)

THE LATER SHU DYNASTY 934 A.D. - 965 A.D.

A governor Mêng Chih Hsiang took the title of Emperor in 934 A.D., having in fact ruled for eight years without the title. On his death in the same year his third son, Mêng Ch'ang became Emperor and ruled until 965 A.D. when he was deposed and the Dynasty came to an end.

THE EMPEROR MÊNG CH'ANG 934 A.D. - 965 A.D.
PERIOD KUANG CHÊNG 938 A.D. - 965 A.D.

No. 301. Legend. KUANG CHÊNG T'UNG PAO (Coinage of the Universal Administration)
Note. This coin seems to have been cast for only one year, 938 A.D.

THE SOUTHERN T'ANG DYNASTY 937 A.D. - 976 A.D.

On the death of the Wu Emperor Jui a certain Hsü Chih-kao, apparently an adopted son became ruler and promptly changed the dynastic title to Nan T'ang, or Southern T'ang. At the same time to make things more confusing he altered his own name to Li Pien but it is as Lieh Tsu, his Temple Title, he is best known. He ruled for six years and was succeeded by his eldest son Yüan Tsung who died in 961 A.D. The throne then passed to Hou Chu, the son of Yüan Tsung, and the dynasty came to an end when he was deposed in 976 A.D. Only the first two Emperors of the Dynasty issued coins.

THE EMPEROR LIEH TSU 937 A.D. - 943 A.D.

No. 302. Legend. K'AI YÜAN T'UNG PAO (Coinage of the Inauguration)
Note. This coin was cast in the year 940 A.D. The legend had been used by earlier rulers, in particular by the T'ang Dynasty, but as the legend of this coin is written in seal script there can be no confusion.

THE EMPEROR YÜAN TSUNG 943 A.D. - 961 A.D.
PERIOD PAO TA 943 A.D. - 958 A.D.

No. 303. Legend. PAO TA YÜAN PAO (Coinage of Great Value)
Note. The characters transliterated by PAO differ so no improper repetition occurs in the legend.
No. 304. Legend TA T'ANG T'UNG PAO (Coinage of the Great T'ang)
Nos. 305-306. Legend. T'ANG KUO T'UNG PAO (Coinage of the State of T'ang)
No. 305. The legend is written in seal script.
No. 306. The legend is written in orthodox characters.
No. 307. Legend YUNG T'UNG CH'ÜAN HUO (Coinage of Unchanging Unity)
Note. This coin was intended to circulate as ten normal cash but its light weight made it unacceptable and it was soon withdrawn.

THE HSIA DYNASTY 982 A.D. - 1227 A.D.

The remnants of the Toba state of the sixth century retreated to the mountainous regions in Kan-Su on the borders of Tibet and there formed a strong military unit rather than a state. Their language would seem to have been Tibetan rather than Chinese. Both the Chinese and the Kitan Tartars, later the Liao Dynasty, angled for an alliance and the old name of Toba was revived in 1031 A.D. and the old dreams of conquest re-awakened. The Sung armies were defeated and an annual levy of fifty thousand dollars in silver demanded and in 1038 A.D. Ching Tsung took to himself the title of Emperor. The province of Shen-Hsi fell to them but a new power was appearing on the Chinese scene, the Mongol forces who were to establish the Yüan Dynasty. The Hsia submitted to them in 1209 A.D. but a misjudged rising in 1227 A.D. led to their annihilation and the name of Toba disappears from history.

THE EMPEROR CH'UNG TSUNG 1087 A.D. - 1139 A.D.
PERIOD YÜAN TÊ 1119 A.D. - 1127 A.D.

No. 308. Legend. YÜAN TÊ T'UNG PAO (Coinage of Approaching Virtue)

Note. Ch'ung Tsung was the great grandson of Ching Tsung who first claimed the title of Emperor.

THE EMPEROR JÊN TSUNG 1139 A.D. - 1193 A.D.
PERIOD T'IEN SHÊNG 1149 A.D. - 1171 A.D.

No. 309. Legend. T'IEN SHÊNG YÜAN PAO (Coinage of Celestial Abundance)

Note. The legend is read in a clockwise direction.

PERIOD CH'IEN YU 1171 A.D. - 1193 A.D.

No. 310. Legend. CH'IEN YU YÜAN PAO (Coinage of Celestial Protection)
Note. The legend of this coin is read in a clockwise direction. During the reign of this Emperor, the eldest son of Ch'ung Tsung, the Hsia reached their greatest expansion of territory.

THE EMPEROR HUAN TSUNG 1193 A.D. - 1206 A.D.
PERIOD T'IEN CH'ING 1194 A.D. - 1206 A.D.

No. 311. Legend. T'IEN CH'ING T'UNG PAO (Coinage of Celestial Benefit)
Note. This Emperor was the eldest son of Jên Tsung.

THE EMPEROR HSIANG TSUNG 1206 A.D. - 1211 A.D.
PERIOD HUANG CHIEN 1210 A.D. - 1211 A.D.

No. 312. Legend. HUANG CHIEN YÜAN PAO (Coinage of the Strong Empire)

Note. The legend of this rare coin is read in a clockwise direction. The Emperor Hsiang Tsung was a nephew of Jên Tsung and so a grandson of Ch'ung Tsung.

THE EMPEROR SHÊN TSUNG 1211 A.D. - 1223 A.D.
PERIOD KUANG TING 1211 A.D. - 1223 A.D.

No. 313. Legend. KUANG TING YÜAN PAO (Coinage of Unchanging Brightness)

Note. The legend of this coin is read in a clockwise direction. This Emperor abdicated in favour of his son Hsien Tsung whose reign lasted barely two years. Soon after the Toba were destroyed by Gengis Khan.

THE LIAO DYNASTY 907 A.D. - 1125 A.D.

The Kitan Tartars, a league of Mongol tribes dominated the regions to north of China by the year 900 A.D. In 937 A.D. they adopted a Chinese name, Liao, for the dynasty to show their claim to rule all China and placed a Turkish general Shih Ching-t'ang on the throne as a puppet ruler. They defeated the Sung forces and exacted an annual levy of a hundred thousand dollars of silver but fell before the Nü Chên Tartars, later the Chin Dynasty. Their name for their country, Kitai, passed on to Europe as Cathay and led to the belief that there were two countries China and

Cathay. It will be remembered that the early explorers of the Americas were seeking Cathay. The remnants of the Kitan Tartars retreated into Turkistan and there formed the state known as the Western Liao.

THE EMPEROR T'AI TSU 907 A.D. - 926 A.D.
PERIOD T'IEN TSAN 922 A.D. - 926 A.D.

No. 314. Legend. T'IEN TSAN T'UNG PAO (Coinage of Heavenly Provision)
Note. The legend is read in a clockwise direction.

THE EMPEROR MU TSUNG 951 A.D. - 969 A.D.
PERIOD YING LI 951 A.D. - 969 A.D.

No. 315. Legend. YING LI T'UNG PAO (Coinage of Period of Correctness)
Note. The legend is read in a clockwise direction.
No. 316. Legend. YING LI CHUNG PAO (Heavy Coinage of the Period of Correctness)
Note. The Emperor Mu Tsung was a grandson of T'ai Tsu.

THE EMPEROR SHÊNG TSUNG 982 A.D. - 1031 A.D.
PERIOD T'UNG HO 983 A.D. - 1012 A.D.

No. 317. Legend. T'UNG HO YÜAN PAO (Coinage of Harmonious Unity)
Note. The legend of this coin is read in a clockwise direction.

PERIOD T'AI P'ING 1021 A.D. - 1031 A.D.

No. 318. Legend. T'AI P'ING YÜAN PAO (Coinage of the Celestial Kingdom)
Note. This coin is of the highest rarity as no specimen exists even in the Museum in Taiwan. During the T'ai P'ing Rebellion (See Nos. 362 - 370) coins using the legend T'AI P'ING were issued but as none of these was Yuan Pao no confusion arises. This emperor was a great great grandson of T'ai Tsu.

THE EMPEROR HSING TSUNG 1031 A.D. - 1055 A.D.
PERIOD CHUNG HSI 1032 A.D. - 1055 A.D.

No. 319. Legend. CHUNG HSI T'UNG PAO (Coinage of Calm Unity)
Note. The legend of this coin is read in a clockwise direction. The Emperor Hsing Tsung was the eldest son of Shêng Tsung.

THE EMPEROR TAO TSUNG 1055 A.D. - 1101 A.D.
PERIOD CH'ING NING 1055 A.D. - 1065 A.D.

No. 320. Legend. CH'ING NING T'UNG PAO (Coinage of Tranquil Clarity)

PERIOD HSIEN YUNG 1065 A.D. - 1075 A.D.

No. 321. Legend. HSIEN YUNG YÜAN PAO (Coinage of Great Peace)

PERIOD TA K'ANG 1075 A.D. - 1085 A.D.

No. 322. Legend. TA K'ANG YÜAN PAO (Coinage of Great Peace)
No. 323. Legend. TA K'ANG T'UNG PAO (Coinage of Great Peace)

PERIOD TA AN 1085 A.D. - 1095 A.D.

No. 324. Legend. TA AN YÜAN PAO (Coinage of Great Calm)

PERIOD SHOU CH'ANG 1095 A.D. - 1101 A.D.

No. 325. Legend. SHOU CH'ANG YÜAN PAO (Coinage of an

Honourable Age)

Note. This Emperor, the eldest son of Hsing Tsung, was the most prolific producer of coinage during this dynasty, changing his Period Title regularly every ten years. On all the coins of this reign the legend is read in a clockwise direction.

THE EMPEROR T'IEN TSO 1101 A.D. - 1125 A.D.
PERIOD CH'IEN T'UNG 1101 A.D. - 1111 A.D.

No. 326. Legend. CH'IEN T'UNG T'UNG PAO (Coinage of Celestial Unity)

Note. The characters transliterated by T'UNG differ so the legend does not contain any improper repetition. The legend is read in a clockwise direction.

PERIOD T'IEN CH'ING 1111 A.D. - 1121 A.D.

No. 327. Legend. T'IEN CH'ING YÜAN PAO (Coinage of Celestial Blessing)

Note. The legend is read in a clockwise direction. This Emperor, a grandson of Tao Tsung also changed his period each ten years. He was deposed in 1124 A.D. and his death the following year brought the Liao Dynasty to a close.

THE CHIN DYNASTY 1115 A.D. - 1234 A.D.

This Dynasty originated in a league of Tungus tribesmen to the north of China. When the Sung Emperor Hui Tsung tired of the annual exactions of the Kitan Tartars, the Liao Dynasty, he formed an alliance with the Nü-Chên Tartars which defeated the Kitans in 1114 A.D. and finally destroyed them eleven years later. In 1114 A.D. the Nü-Chên leader A Ku Ta assumed the title of Emperor, later known as T'ai Tsu, and called the Dynasty the Chin, the Golden Dynasty. In 1126 A.D. the Chinese capital and the last of the Northern section of the Sung Dynasty fell into their hands and a campaign was mounted to complete the conquest of China by crossing the Yangtse. However an organisation which was admirably suited for a tribal confederation failed when put to the test of governing so large an area and the Chin forces had to retreat to the northern banks of the river. Failure to integrate the native Chinese into their empire sowed the seeds of dissolution and even their military success failed them when they attacked the Mongols, the Yüan Dynasty of later years. Gengis Khan became ruler of the Mongols in 1189 A.D. and having destroyed the Hsia turned his attention to the Chin. The key points guarding the frontiers fell to his troops and in 1234 A.D. the Chin Dynasty was utterly destroyed. The remnants retreated into Manchuria to make another appearance on the stage of Chinese history in the seventeenth century as the Manchu Dynasty, the Ch'ing, the last to rule over the Empire of China.

THE EMPEROR FEI TI 1150 A.D. - 1161 A.D.
PERIOD CHÊNG LUNG 1156 A.D. - 1161 A.D.

No. 328. Legend CHÊNG LUNG YÜAN PAO (Coinage of Eminent Probity)

Note. The legend on these coins of Fei Ti, the fourth Emperor of the Dynasty, is read in a clockwise direction. Although no mint name appears on the reverse these coins were cast at the two mints at Chang-tu in Shan-Tung and Ching-pei in Shan-Hsi.

THE EMPEROR SHIH TSUNG 1161 A.D. - 1189 A.D.
PERIOD TA TING 1161 A.D. - 1189 A.D.

No. 329. Legend TA TING T'UNG PAO (Coinage of Great Calm)
Note. On the reverse of some coins of this issue appear the cyclical characters Shen or Yu, indicating the years 1188 A.D. and 1189 A.D. respectively. Shih Tsung was a grandson of T'au Tsu the first Emperor of the Dynasty.

THE EMPEROR CHANG TSUNG 1189 A.D. - 1208 A.D.
PERIOD CH'ÊNG AN 1196 A.D. - 1201 A.D.

No. 330. Legend CH'ÊNG AN PAO HUO (Precious Coinage of Beneficial Peace)

PERIOD T'AI HO 1201 A.D. - 1208 A.D.

No. 331. Legend. T'AI HO T'UNG PAO (Coinage of Honourable Peace)
Note. The reverse types of this coin are many and varied as it was used for centuries as an amulet. Gods, birds and beasts appear and on a rare variety the obverse legend appears on the reverse inverted.

No.332. Legend T'AI HO CHUNG PAO (Heavy Coinage of Honourable Peace)
Note. Chang Tsung was a grandson of the previous Emperor Shih Tsung.

THE EMPEROR HSÜAN TSUNG 1213 A.D. - 1224 A.D.
PERIOD CHÊNG YU 1213 A.D. - 1217 A.D.

No. 333. Legend. CHÊNG YU T'UNG PAO (Coinage of Protecting Virtue)
Note. Hsüan Tsung, the last Emperor of this dynasty to issue coins, was another grandson of the Emperor Shih Tsung.

THE COINAGE OF PRETENDERS AND REBELS.

P'ei Wang Circa 160 B.C.
Tung Che Circa 190 A.D. - 200 A.D.
Shih Ssu Ming 759 A.D. - 761 A.D.
Ma Yin 927 A.D. - 930 A.D.
Tsao Wang 1130 A.D. - 1137 A.D.
Rebels at the close of the Yüan Dynasty 1355 A.D. - 1367 A.D.
Ming Pretenders and Rebels 1639 A.D. - 1681 A.D.
The T'ai P'ing Rebellion 1850 A.D. - 1864 A.D.

THE COINAGE OF REBELS AND PRETENDERS

Between 160 B.C. and 1864 A.D. some two dozen rebel leaders issued coinage with attributable legends. The coins of the rebel leader Kung Sun Shih circa 24 A.D. - 36 A.D. have been listed under No.22 as they are merely variants of the issues of the Usurper Wang Mang but all other coins issued by pretenders and rebels will be found in this section.

THE FEUDAL STATE OF WU
P'EI WANG circa 160 B.C.

No. 334. Legend LIANG TCHE (Double Tche)
Note. The Tche weight was a quarter of a Liang so a double Tche was the same weight as the Pan Liang coinage described in No.1 et seq.

THE REBEL TUNG CHO circa 190 A.D. - 200 A.D.

No. 335. Legend. Blank.
Note. Tung Cho was an adventurer who had Hsien Ti (189 A.D. - 220 A.D.) enthroned as a nine year old puppet emperor. In place of the Wu Chu coins then in issue he had metal discs cast which lacked both rims and legends. While in design it represents the lowest point ever reached by the copper cash of China its weight, varying from 20 to 35 grams, probably made it readily acceptable by the common people who were completely incapable of reading the legend on a coin and probably completely disinterested in anything but the weight of metal contained in it.

THE REBEL SHIH SSU MING 759 A.D. - 761 A.D.

Under the title of Yen Wang, Prince of Yen, this rebel ruled most of North East China with his capital at Cheng-tu.

No. 336. Legend TÊ YI YÜAN PAO (Coinage of Unity)
Note. This coin, issued in 759 A.D. was intended to circulate at a value of one hundred of the K'ai Yüan coins of the T'ang Dynasty. As its weight was barely six normal cash it was soon withdrawn, allegedly because its legend was unlucky,„and replaced by the next coin.

No. 337. Legend SHUN T'IEN YÜAN PAO (Coinage Agreeable to Heaven)
Note. While slightly heavier than the previous coin the weight was still in no way compatable with a valuation of a hundred cash and its period of issue was very short.

THE REBEL STATE OF CH'U 927 A.D. - 953 A.D.
PRINCE MA YIN 927 A.D. - 930 A.D.

No. 338. Legend T'IEN TS'Ê FU PAO (Coinage of T'ien Ts'ê Prefecture)
Note. On the reverse is the character YIN referring to Ma Yin. These coins weigh a full eighteen grams and probably circulated as ten cash.

No. 339. Legend. CH'IEN FÊNG CH'ÜAN PAO (Exchange Coinage of Celestial Protection)
Note. On the reverse is the mint name of T'ien Ts'ê Prefecture, the principality of Ma Yin. With a weight of thirty grams these coins represent a full ten cash coin but probably circulated at a much higher value. This legend had also been used by the T'ang Emperor Kao Tsung (See No. 61) but the larger size of Ma Yin's issue and the reverse mint name prevent any confusion.

THE REBEL STATE OF CH'I 1130 A.D. - 1137 A.D.
TSAO WANG 1130 A.D. - 1137 A.D.
PERIOD FOU CH'ANG- 1130 A.D. - 1137 A.D.

No. 340. Legend. FOU CH'ANG YÜAN PAO (Coinage of Fou Ch'ang)
Note. The legend of this rare coin is written in seal script.

No. 341. Legend. FOU CH'ANG T'UNG PAO (Coinage of Fou Ch'ang)
Note. The legend of this coin is also written in seal script.
Tsoa Wang was a rebel against the Sung Dynasty. Allying himself with the Nü Chên Tartars, the Chin Dynasty, he was rewarded by being made a puppet Emperor, only to be deposed after seven years when his usefulness had ceased. These two coins attributable to him are very rare, probably only a token issue having been cast.

REBELS AT THE CLOSE OF THE YÜAN DYNASTY 1355 A.D. - 1367 A.D.

With the breakup of the Yüan Dynasty several war lords and rebels strove for the throne of China. A glance at the dates of these rebels who failed in the attempt will show how quickly T'ai Tsu established his control over the country and set up the Ming Dynasty.

HAN LIN ÊRH 1355 A.D. - 1367 A.D.
PERIOD LUNG FÊNG 1355 A.D. - 1367 A.D.

No. 342. Legend. LUNG FÊNG T'UNG PAO (Coinage of Changing Strength)
Note. Han Lin, who claimed descent from the Sung Emperors, seized Ngan-Hui (An-Hui) Province in 1355 A.D. and held out against the Ming armies until 1367 A.D. making the city of Po-chao his capital.

CHANG SHI CH'ÊNG 1353 A.D. - 1367 A.D.
PERIOD T'IEN HO 1353 A.D. - 1367 A.D.

No. 343. Legend. T'IEN HO T'UNG PAO (Coinage of Celestial Harmony)
Note. Chang Shi Ch'êng claimed descent from the Emperors of the Later Chou Dynasty and based on the city of Yang-chao in Chiang-Su Province died undefeated in 1367 A.D. Starting life as he had done as a merchant he appreciated the need for a satisfactory coinage and did not hesitate to plunder the Buddhist monasteries of their statues to provide the necessary metal. His coinage, which varies considerably in diameter, was issued in two values, one and five cash coins, the latter having the numeral WU on the reverse.

CH'ÊN YU LIANG 1360 A.D. - 1363 A.D.
PERIOD T'IEN CH'I 1358 A.D. - 1359 A.D.

No. 344. Legend. T'IEN CH'I T'UNG PAO (Coinage of Celestial Beginning)
Note. This coin was cast before Ch'ên Yu Liang actually claimed the title of Emperor in 1360 A.D. This legend also appears on a coin of the Ming Emperor Hsi Tsung (See No. 262). The coins of this fourteenth century issue may be distinguished by the upper cross stroke of the character T'IEN being much shorter than the lower cross stroke.

PERIOD TA I 1360 A.D.

No. 345. Legend. TA I T'UNG PAO (Coinage of Great Unity)

PERIOD T'IEN TING 1361 A.D. - 1363 A.D.

No. 346. Legend. T'IEN TING T'UNG PAO (Coinage of Celestial Calm)
Note. Ch'ên Yu Liang claimed descent from the Han Dynasty and entitled his own line TA HAN, Great Han. Before his death in 1363 A.D. he had captured and successfully defended the cities of Wu-Chang and Nan-king.

MING YU CHEN 1363 A.D. - 1367 A.D.

No. 347. Legend. T'IEN T'UNG YÜAN PAO (Coinage of Celestial Unity)
Note. Ming Yu Chen, who took the title of the Ruler of Hsia, died in 1367 A.D. the last to oppose T'ai Tsu for the throne of China. The legend of his coinage is written in seal script.

MING PRETENDERS AND REBELS 1639 A.D. - 1681 A.D.

With the breaking up of the Ming Dynasty ten Pretenders and rebels attempted to seize what looked like an empty throne and their coins are listed from No. 348 to No. 361. Every kind of Ming Pretender, War Lord and traitor played their part in the stormy scenes leading up to the success of the Manchus and their coins make an interesting section.

LU WANG 1644 A.D. - 1657 A.D.

No. 348. Legend. TA MING T'UNG PAO (Coinage of Great Ming)
Note. Lu Wang, the only real hope of the Ming faction failed in his attempt to capture Che-kiang in 1657 A.D. and as usually happens to unsuccessful Rebels his following melted away. On the reverse of his coinage will be found the mint names of the Board of Revenue Mint and the Board of Works Mint. Some coins have on the reverse either the numeral one or two, perhaps indicating the date of issue.

FU WANG 1644 A.D. - 1645 A.D.
PERIOD HUNG KUANG 1645 A.D.

No. 349. Legend. HUNG KUANG T'UNG PAO (Coinage of Great Lustre)
Note. Fu Wang claimed to be the son of the Ming Emperor Kuang Tsung, whence perhaps comes his Period Title. He claimed the Imperial Title in 1644 A.D. and died a year later. The only mint name to appear on his coinage is that of Feng-yang in Ngan-Hui (An-Hui) Province.

T'ANG WANG 1645 A.D. - 1646 A.D.
PERIOD LUNG WU 1645 A.D. - 1646 A.D.

No. 350. Legend. LUNG WU T'UNG PAO (Coinage of Exalted Prowess)
Note. T'ang Wang claimed descent from T'ai Tsu, the founder of the Ming Dynasty and set up his standard at Foo-chao. He was defeated and died in 1646 A.D. On the reverse of his coins will be found the mint names of the Board of Revenue Mint and the Board of Works Mint.

YUNG MING WANG 1646 A.D. - 1662 A.D.
PERIOD YUNG LI 1647 A.D. - 1662 A.D.

Nos.351-353. Legend YUNG LI T'UNG PAO (Coinage of the Everlasting Succession)
No. 351. The legend is written in seal script.
No. 352. The legend is written in orthodox characters.
No. 353. The legend is written in the cursive style of writing.
Note. Prince Yung Ming, like Fu Wang a grandson of the Ming Emperor Shên Tsung, proclaimed himself Emperor at Chao-ch'ing and was shortly afterwards defeated by a Manchu army in Yun-Nan and retreated into Burma. In later years he became a Christian and it is one of the imponderables of history as to the outcome of a Christian Dynasty in China at that time had he won. Coins valued at one, two and five cash were issued bearing on the reverse the mint names of either the Board of Revenue Mint or the Board of Works Mint. The reverse of the coins with orthodox characters were used to publish a declaration, one character per coin, and are known as the Declaration Coins. The Declaration was...YU CHIH TU PU TAO FU LIU YUEH FU MING TING KUO (The Governors General, the Tao Tais, and the Prefects are charged by the Emperor to guard Kuang-

Tung and Kuang-Hsi and to assist Ming to settle the State.) The characters are to be found in Appendix D.

LI TSU CHENG 1644 A.D. - 1645 A.D.

No. 354. Legend. YUNG CH'ANG T'UNG PAO (Coinage of Everlasting Prosperity)
Note. These coins were issued in two values, one and five cash. Some of them have on the reverse the cyclical character YI (One) apparently to indicate 1644 A.D., the first year of issue. Li Tsu Cheng took the opportunity given to him when General Wu San Kwei moved his army from Pekin to oppose the advancing Manchu forces and seized the capital. Chuang Lieh Ti, the last Ming Emperor hanged himself in despair and Li Tsu Cheng declared himself Emperor. He had the family of General Wu San Kwei murdered and when he heard of this the General allied his army with the Manchus and recaptured Pekin. Li Tsu Cheng retreated into Shen-Hsi Province but was soon overtaken and he and his family were killed, a just and swift retribution. The coins issued by General Wu San Kwei will be found described under Nos. 357 - 359

CHANG HSIEN CHUNG 1639 A.D. - 1644 A.D.

No. 355. Legend. TA SHUN T'UNG PAO (Coinage of Great Compliance)
Note. The reverse of some of these coins bears the mint names of the Board of Revenue or the Board of Works. The numerals one or two also sometimes appear, probably indicating the year of issue. Chang Hsien Chung was a War Lord based on Cheng-tu, the capital city of Ssu-Ch'uan Province. In 1644 A.D. he claimed the title of Emperor but his ' reign ' was a short one as a Manchu army ended his claims and his life that same year. His passing can have been mourned by few as in a profession noted for the extortion and rapacity displayed by those who aspired to succeed he was known as the most brutal ruffian ever to disgrace the history of a civilised country.

SUN KO WANG 1645 A.D. - 1660 A.D.

No. 356. Legend. HSING CH'AO T'UNG PAO (Coinage of the Rising Dynasty)
Note. Some of these coins have the mint name of the Board of Works Mint on the reverse. Sun Ko was the adopted son of Chang Hsien Chung (See No. 355) and after his death led the remnants of his army into Yun-Nan Province where these coins were cast in 1655 A.D. After a few years precarious existence as a War Lord in the remoter parts of Yun-Nan he made his peace with the Manchus and ended his days in Pekin as a closely watched pensioner.

WU SAN KWEI 1644 A.D. - 1678 A.D.

No. 357. Legend LI YUNG T'UNG PAO (Coinage of the Li Yung Mint)
Note. On the reverse of some of these coins appear the mint names of Yun-Nan and Kwei-chau. Wu San Kwei was a Chinese General who allied his army with the Manchus in order to avenge himself after Li Tsu Cheng (See No. 354) had murdered his family. As a reward he was made Governor of Yun-Nan where this coin was cast. In 1674 A.D. he proclaimed himself Emperor and for the four years before his death had the following coins issued.

PERIOD CH'AO WU 1674 A.D. - 1678 A.D.

Nos. 358-359. Legend. CH'AO WU T'UNG PAO (Coinage of Brilliant Success)

No. 358. The legend is written in seal script.
No. 359. The legend is written in orthodox characters.
Note. Some of the coins with the legend written in orthodox characters have on the reverse the mint name of the Board of Works Mint.

WU SHIH FAN 1678 A.D. - 1681 A.D.

No. 360. Legend HUNG HUA T'UNG PAO (Coinage of Extensive Reform)
Note. The mint names of the Board of Revenue and the Board of Works appear on the reverse of some coins of this issue. Also to be found are the numerals one or two, probably indicating 1678 A.D. or 1679 A.D. Wu Shih Fan succeeded his father Wu San Kwei (See Nos. 357 - 359) as leader of the Ming insurgents in Yun-Nan and in the three years before his death had the above coin cast. From the absence of coins bearing the numeral three it would seem that minting ceased after 1679 A.D.

KÊNG CHING CHUNG 1676 A.D. - 1681 A.D.

No. 361. Legend. YÜ MIN T'UNG PAO (Coinage to Enrich the People)
Note. On the reverse of most of these coins, cast in 1676 A.D. will be found the mint name of Che-Chiang. Kêng Ching Chung was the last of those who endeavoured to restore the fortunes of the Ming Dynasty.

Collectors will experience little difficulty in obtaining a representative selection of the coins cast by the Ming Rebels and Pretenders though certain mint names and numerals are more scarce than others. A complete set, however, of the Declaration Coins will be the most difficult to complete.

THE T'AI P'ING REBELLION 1850 A.D. - 1864 A.D.

The T'ai P'ing rising was a very complex affair and more of an attempted revolution than a rebellion. Hung Hsui Ch'uan, a scholar who had failed to pass the requisite examinations to enter the official classes, went into a trance some time after reading a missionary tract and became convinced that he was the Son of God. Rousing the people of South China against the Manchus he captured Nan-king in 1850 A.D. and proclaimed himself T'ien Wang, Prince of Heaven, and for dynastic title chose the boastful T'ai P'ing Tien Kuo, The Heavenly Kingdom of Great Peace. Preaching purity and the communal ownership of property he appealed to the Chinese peasantry and for some time seemed likely to oust the Manchus from the Imperial Throne. However success brought in its train corruption and as he lost the support of the common people the Manchu armies led by foreign mercenaries, General Ward, an American killed in a battle near Ning-po in 1862 A.D., and then General Gordon, who was to die when Khartoum fell to the forces of the Mahdi, defeated his forces and in 1864 A.D. recaptured Nan-king. Hung Hsui Ch'uan committed suicide but the unrest in China which had almost swept him to Pekin was not stilled and culminated some fifty years later in the revolution which brought the Republic of China into being. The more immediate results of this rebellion was the destruction of six hundred cities and the deaths of more than twenty million people. The economic results of the upheaval in China during this time was the casting of both Depreciated cash and so called Heavy cash, both in reality token coinages.

HUNG HSUI CH'UAN 1850 A.D. - 1864 A.D.

No. 362. Legend. T'AI P'ING T'UNG PAO (Coinage of Great Peace) Note. Some of these coins will have on the reverse the mint names of Fu-Chien or Yun-Nan Provinces, the strongholds of the T'ai P'ing rebels. The others bear on the reverse the character MING. These last were issued by the forces of Liu Li Ch'üan which captured Shanghai in 1853 A.D. This obverse legend was also used by the Sung Dynasty (See No. 79) but as the Sung coins have blank reverses there can be no confusion.

No. 363. Legend T'AI P'ING T'IEN KUO (The Heavenly Kingdom of Great Peace)
Note. Two types of reverse are known of this issue. The first has the characters SHÊNG PAO (Sacred Coin) to the right and left of the aperture while on the second type they appear above and below the aperture.

No. 364. Legend. T'AI P'ING SHÊNG PAO (Sacred Coinage of Great Peace)
Note. On the reverse of the coins of this issue appear the characters T'IEN KUO (Heavenly Kingdom)

No. 365. Legend HUANG TI T'UNG PAO (Coinage of the Empire) Note. There are two reverse types. On the first appears the character SHÊNG (Sacred) while the second has to the left of the aperture BOO (PAO in Manchu) and the mint name of Che-Chiang Province to the right, also in Manchu. The use of Manchu writing on this second type is rather surprising as the T'ai P'ing rebels stressed that their movement was for the end of the Manchu rule and a return to the Chinese rule of the Ming.

No. 366. Legend T'AI P'ING CHÊNG PAO (True Coinage of Great Peace)
Note. This is perhaps the most uncommon type of coin issued by the T'ai P'ing rebels and the legend seems to suggest that counterfeiting, never far distant in China, had become a pressing problem.

No. 367. Legend T'IEN KUO (Heavenly Kingdom)
Note. On the reverse are the characters SHÊNG PAO (Sacred Coinage). This heavy coin circulated as ten cash and is rather rare.

No. 368. Legend. T'IEN KUO SHÊNG PAO (Sacred Coinage of the Heavenly Kingdom)

No. 369. Legend. NAN WANG T'UNG PAO (Coinage of the Southern Prince)
Note. Since Nan Wang, the Southern Prince, was one of the titles Hung Hsui Ch'uan bestowed on himself this coin must belong to the T'ai P'ing series.

No. 370. Legend. T'IEN KUO T'AI P'ING (Great Peace of the Heavenly Kingdom)
Note. On the reverse appear the characters SHÊNG PAO (Sacred Coinage). This coin has the same legend as No. 363 with the characters in a different order.

APPENDICES

A Summary of Pan Liang and Wu Chu coins

B The metal used in the coinage.

C Reverse marks in Chinese

D MINT MARKS IN MANCHU

E Numerals etc.

F Illustrations of Obverse types

SUMMARY OF PAN LIANG VARIETIES

No. 1. Diameter 40 - 28 mms. Inner rim.

No. 2. Diameter 20 - 10 mms.

No. 3. Diameter 32 - 25 mms.

No. 4. Diameter 27 - 24 mms. Weight of an average cash coin.

No. 5. Diameter 25 mms. Rudimentary outer rim.

SUMMARY OF WU CHU VARIETIES

(a) Square outline of character CHU - from about 100 B.C.-200 A.D.

(b) Rounded outline of character CHU - from about 200 A.D.-600 A.D.

No. 9. Raised rim above obverse aperture.

No.22. An iron coin with straight cross strokes of character CHU

No.23. No inner rim on the obverse.

No.24. Similar to No.23 with short diagonal rays on obverse and reverse.

No.33. A very small coin, diameter 16 mms, with incomplete legends.

No.36. A heavy coin with a prominent rim.

No.42. Outer and inner rims on both obverse and reverse.

No.43. A coin lacking outer and inner rims on obverse and reverse.

No.44. A small coin with legends cramped between the aperture and edge.

No.45. A coin lacking part of the character CHU.

No.46. An iron coin with diagonal rays on the reverse.

No.59. A coin, light in colour, with straight diagonal strokes on the character WU.

THE METAL USED IN THE COINAGE

The metal most commonly used in the Chinese cash series is an alloy of copper. At times however iron was used, sometimes with iron coins equalling copper in value and at others with the iron coins having a lower value than copper.

COINS KNOWN ONLY IN IRON

Nos. 164, 165, 175, 178, 180, 183, 184, 185, 186, 187, 188, 189, 190, 191, 192, 193, 194, 195, 196, 197, 198, 199.

COINS KNOWN IN BOTH IRON AND COPPER ALLOY.

Nos. 3, 26, 47, 53, 78, 79, 87, 88, 90, 91, 92, 96, 97, 98, 118, 121, 123, 124, 125, 126, 127, 131, 132, 133, 134, 135, 137, 139, 140, 146, 147, 148, 149, 150, 151, 152, 153, 156, 157, 158, 159, 160, 161, 162, 163, 168, 172, 177, 179, 200, 202, 203, 204, 273, 274, 275, 277, 284, 328, 329.

Note. In some cases where the coin exists in both iron and copper alloy the latter is a trial piece and consequently rare. Perhaps in the future collectors will find more of these and some of the numbers in the list of iron coins will have to be transferred to the second list. A silver example of one of the Ch'ing Dynasty issues is known, probably a presentation piece, and again in the future more of these will be discovered. I may mention here that Chinese numismatists are highly appreciative of the iron coinage and when the collector discovers how difficult it is to obtain examples in collectable condition he will share their appreciation.

CHARACTERS

REVERSE MARKS (CHINESE)

1. CHANG Chang-chao in Fu-Chien
2. CH'ANG (a) Period title No. 70 (b) Wu-chang in Hu-Pei
3. CHÊ Che-Chiang Province
4. CHÊN Chen-ting in Chih-Li
5. CHI Shan-Tung Province
6. CHI Chi-chao in Chih-Li
7. CHIA Chia-ting in Ssu-Ch'uan
8. CHIANG Nan-king
9. CHING (a) Ching-chao in Ho-Nan (b) Nan-king
10. CH'IN Second character on Declaration Coin No. 352.
11. CHING Ching-chou in Hu-Pei.
12. CH'ING Ching-chao in Shan-Tung.
13. CHI UNG Chiung District in Ssu-Ch'uan
14. CHUAN Cheng-tu in Ssu-Ch'uan
15. HSI (a) Ch'uan-hsi in Ssu-Ch'uan (b) Shan-Hsi Province
16. CH'ÜAN Yen-chao in Che-Chiang
17. CH'UN Chi-chun (Orthodox Characters)
18. CH'UN Chi-chun (Seal Script)
19. CHUNG Chung-ching in Ssu-Ch'uan
20. CHUNG Chung-chao in Ssu-Ch'uan

Reverse characters (Chinese).

21. FENG Feng-yang in Ngan-Hui (An-Hui) Province.

22. FU (a) Hsuan Fu Cheng in Ngan-Hui (An-Hui)
(b) Sixth character of Declaration Coin No. 352.

23. FU Fu-Chien Province

24. FU Fu-Chien Province

25. FU Ninth character of Declaration Coin No. 352.

26. HAN Han-yang in Hu-Pei.

27. HO Ho-Nan Province.

28. HSIANG Hsiang-chou in Chih-Li

29. HSIANG Hsiang-yang in Hu-Pei.

30. HSING Feng-hsiang in Shan-Hsi.

31. HSÜAN (a) Kuang-tê in Ngan-Hui. (b) Hsuan-fu in Chih-Li.

32. HU Board of Revenue Mint.

33. HUI Hui-min.

34. HUNG Lin-kiang in Chiang-Hsi.

35. KUANG (a) Kuang-chao in Kuang-Tung (b) Kuang-Tung Province.

36. KWEI Kwei-chao in Yun-Nan.

37. KWEI Kwei-lin in Kuang-Hsi.

38. KUNG Board of Works Mint.

39. KUNG Kung-cheng in Chih-Li.

40. KUO Last character on Declaration Coin No. 352.

21 22 23 24
25 26 27 28
29 30 31 32
33 34 35 36
37 38 39 40

41.	LAN	Lan-tien in Shan-Hsi.
42.	LI	Li Chao, a district in Shen-Hsi and Ssu-Ch'uan
43.	LIANG	Liang-chau in Hu-Pei.
44.	LIN	Lin-ching in Shan-Tung.
45.	LIU	Seventh character of Declaration Coin No. 352.
46.	LO	Lo-yang in Ho-Nan.
47.	LÜ	Lu-chao in Ssu-Ch'uan
48.	MI	Shun-tien in Chih-Li.
49.	MING	(a) Tenth character of Declaration Coin No. 352.
		(b) The Ming Dynasty No. 362.
50.	NAN	Hu-Nan Province.
51.	NING	Ning-po in Che-Chiang.
52.	O	Wu-chang in Hu-Pei.
53.	PEI P'ING	Pei-p'ing in Chih-Li
54.	P'ING	(a) Yung-ping in Chih-Li (b) Tai-ping in Kuang-Hsi.
55.	PU	Fourth character of Declaration Coin No. 352.
56.	SHEN	Shen-Hsi Province.
57.	SHÊNG	'Holy', on coins of the T'ai P'ing Rebellion.
58.	SU	(a) Su-chao in Chiang-Su (b) Chiang-Su Province.
59.	T'AI P'ING	Tai-ping in Chiang-Hsi.
60.	T'AI	Taiwan Province (The island once called Formosa)

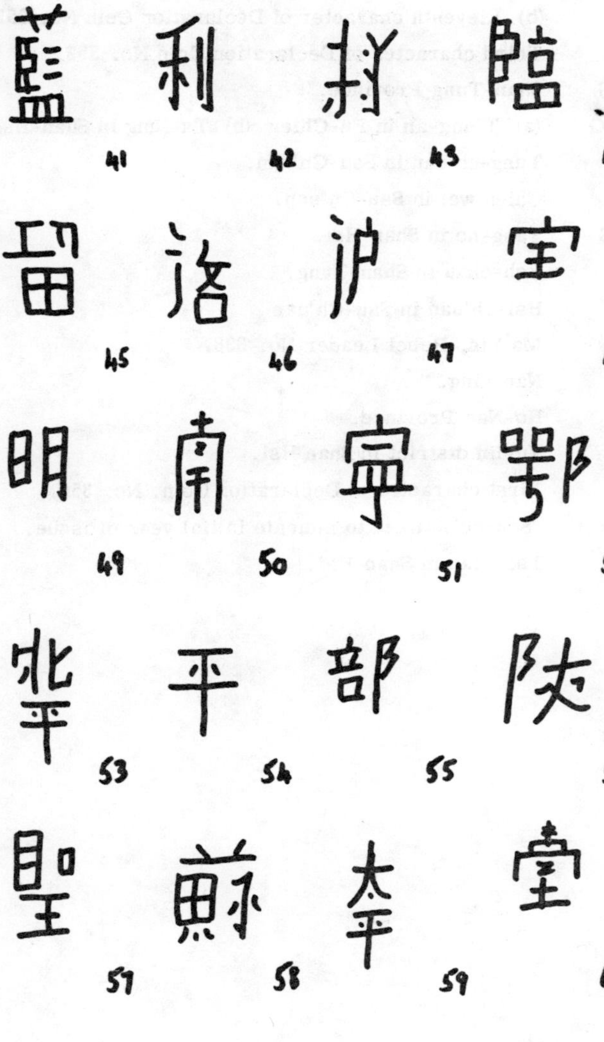
41
42
43
44
45
46
47
48
49
50
51
52
53
54
55
56
57
58
59
60

61.	T'AN	T'an-yang in Hu-Nan.
62.	TAN	Tung-chau in Shen-Hsi.
63.	TAO	Fifth character of Declaration Coin No. 352.
64.	T'IEN	T'ien-tse.
65.	TING	(a) Ting-cheng in Kuang-Tung.
		(b) Eleventh character of Declaration Coin No. 352.
66.	TU	Third character of Declaration Coin No. 352.
67.	TUNG	Shan-Tung Province.
68.	T'UNG	(a) T'ung-an in Fu-Chien (b) Ta-tung in Shan-Hsi.
69.	TZU	Tung-ch'uan in Ssu-Ch'uan.
70.	WEI	Chien wei in Ssu-Ch'uan.
71.	YANG	Yang-ho in Shan-Hsi.
72.	YEN	Yen-chau in Shan-Tung.
73.	YI	Hsi-ch'uan in Ssu-Ch'uan
74.	YIN	Ma Yin, Rebel Leader No. 338.
75.	YING	Nan-king.
76.	YÜ	Ho-Nan Province.
77.	YÜ	Yu-lin district in Shan-Hsi.
78.	YÜ	First character of Declaration Coin. No. 352.
79.	YÜAN	'Source'. Used to indicate initial year of issue.
80.	YÜAN	Tai-yuan in Shan-Hsi.

潭	丹	道	天
61	62	63	64
定	督	東	同
65	66	67	68
梓	為	開	究
69	70	71	72
益	殷	應	豫
73	74	75	76
榆	御	元	原
77	78	79	80

81. YÜEH Yu-chau in Che-Chiang.

82. YÜEH Eighth character of Declaration Coin No. 352.

83. YUN Chen-kiang in Chiang-Su.

84. YÜN Mi-yun in Chih-Li

85. YÜN Yun-Nan Province.

REVERSE CHARACTERS (MONGOL) YÜAN DYNASTY COINS

1. MAO

2. or 3. SSU

4. SHEN

5. CHI (One hundred)

6. The numeral two.

7. The numeral three.

8. The numeral ten.

81 82 83 84 85

Reverse characters (Mongol)

(Yüan Dynasty)

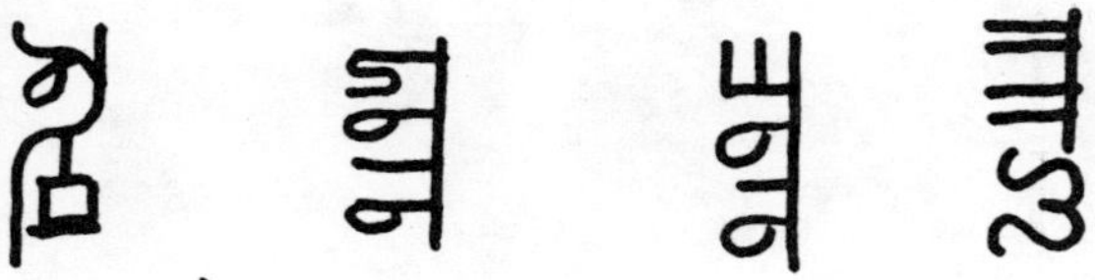

1 2 3 4

5 6 7 8

MINT NAMES (MANCHU)

1. Aksu in Sin-Kiang.
2. Board of Revenue Mint.
3. Board of Works Mint.
4. Chang-chao in Fu-Chien.
5. Ch'ang-te.
6. Che-Chiang Province.
7. Chi-chao in Chih-Li.
8. Chih-Li Province.
9. Chin-an Fu.
10. (a) and (b) Fu-Chien Province.
11. Ho-Nan Province.
12. Hsuan Fu.
13. Hu-Nan Province.
14. Ili, a district of Sin-Kiang.
15. Kwei-chao in Yun-Nan.
16. Kuang-Tung Province.

Mint names (Manchu)

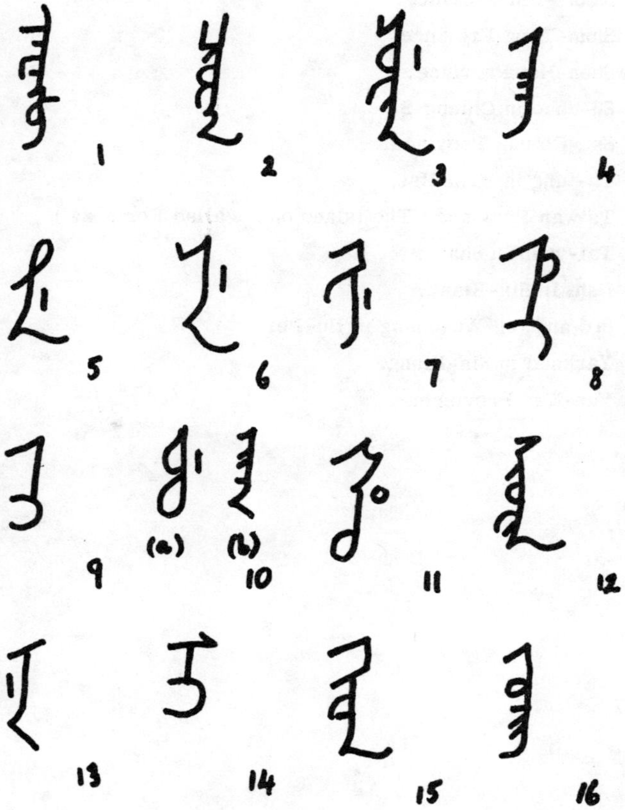

17. Kwei-lin in Kuang-Hsi.
18. Kung-chang.
19. Kuchar in Sin-Kiang
20. Lin-ching in Shan-Tung.
21. Nan-chang.
22. Nan-king.
23. Ngan-hui (An-Hui) Province.
24. Ning-po in Che-Chiang
25. Shan - Hsi Province.
26. Shan-Tung Province.
27. Shen-Hsi Province.
28. Su-chao in Chiang-Su.
29. Ssu-Ch'uan Province.
30. Ta-tung in Shan-Hsi.
31. Taiwan Province (The island once called Formosa) .
32. Tai-yuan in Shan-Hsi.
33. Ushi in Sin-Kiang.
34. (a) and (b) Wu-chang in Hu-Pei.
35. Yarkand in Sin-Kiang.
36. Yun-Nan Province.

17
18
19
20
21
22
23
24
25
26
27
28
29
30
31
32
33
(a)
(b)
34
35
36

Chinese Numerals

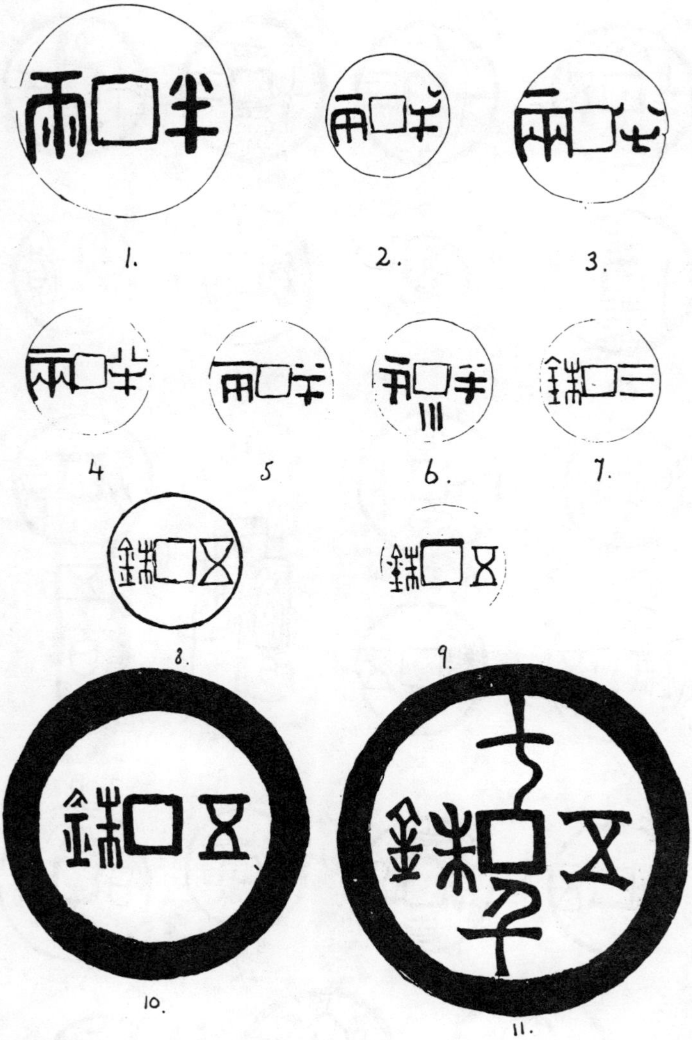
1.
2.
3.
4
5
6.
7.
8.
9.
10.
11.

12

13

14

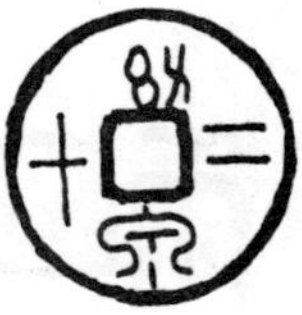
15

16

17.

18

19.

20

21

22.

23

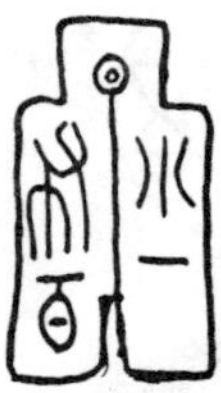
A.

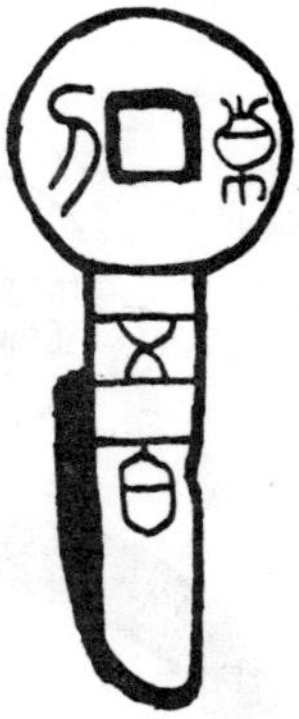
B.

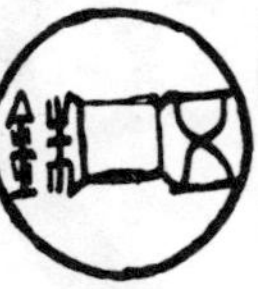
24

25

26.

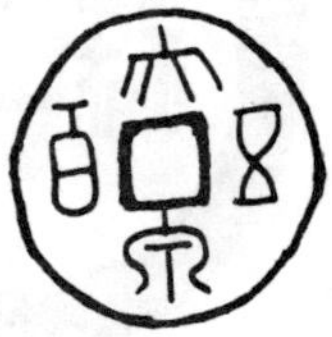
27.

28

29

30

31.

32.

33.

34.

35.

36

37. 38. 41.

39.

40.

42.

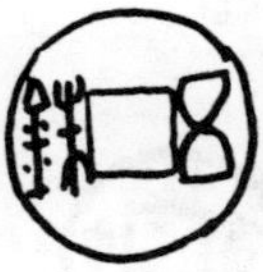
43.

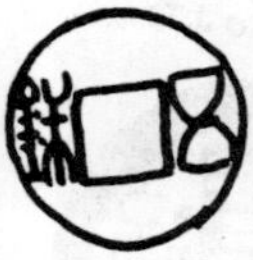
44.

45.

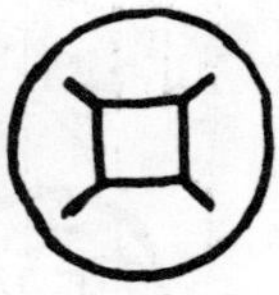
46 (Rev.).

47.

48.

49.

50.

51.

52.

53.

54.

55.

56.

57.

58.

59.

60 & 70

61.

62 – 64.

65.

66.

67.

68.

69.

71.

72.

73.

74.

75.

76.

77.

78.

79.

80.

81.

82.

83.

84.

85.

86.

87.

88.

89.

90.

91.

92.

93.

94.

95.

96.

97.

98

99.

100.

101

102.

103.

104.

105.

106.

107.

108

109.

110.

111.

112.

113.

114.

115.

116.

117.

118.

119.

120.

121.

122.

123.

124.

125.

126

127.

128.

129.

130

131

132

133.

134.

135.

136.

137.

138

139

140

141

142

143

144

145

146

147

148

149

150

151

152

153

154

155

156

157

158

159

160

161.

162

163

164

165

166

167

168

169

170

171

172

173

174

175

176

177

178

179

180

181

182

183

184

185

186

187

188

189.

190

191

192

193

194

195

196

197.

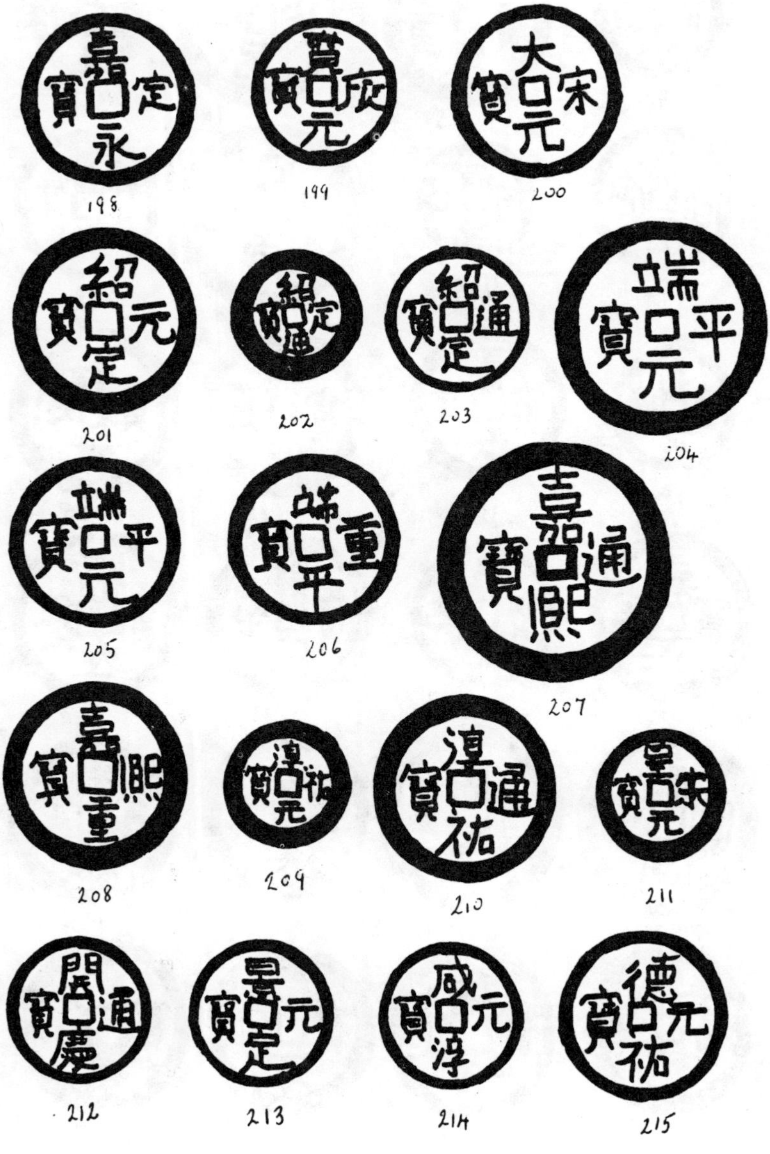
198
199
200
201
202
203
204
205
206
207
208
209
210
211
212
213
214
215

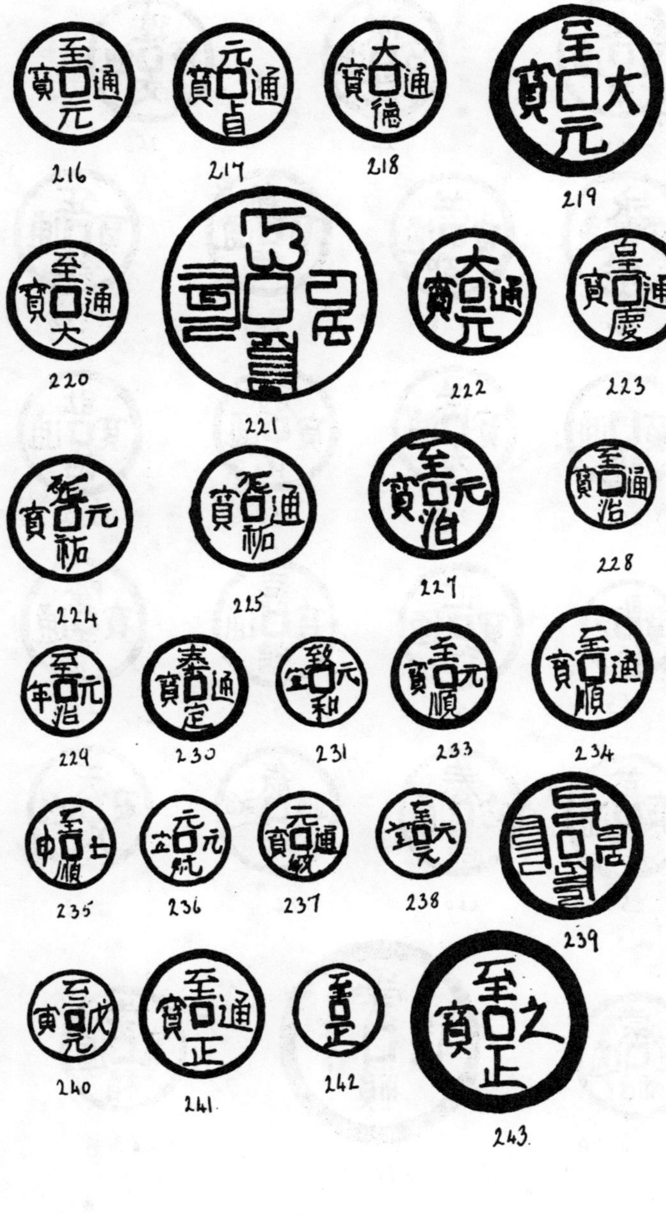
216
217
218
219
220
221
222
223
224
225
227
228
229
230
231
233
234
235
236
237
238
239
240
241
242
243

244

245

246

247

248

249

250

251

252

253

254

255

256

257

258

259

260

261

262

263 A.

264

263 B

265

266

267

268

269

270

271

272

273

274

275

276

277

278

279

280

281

282

283

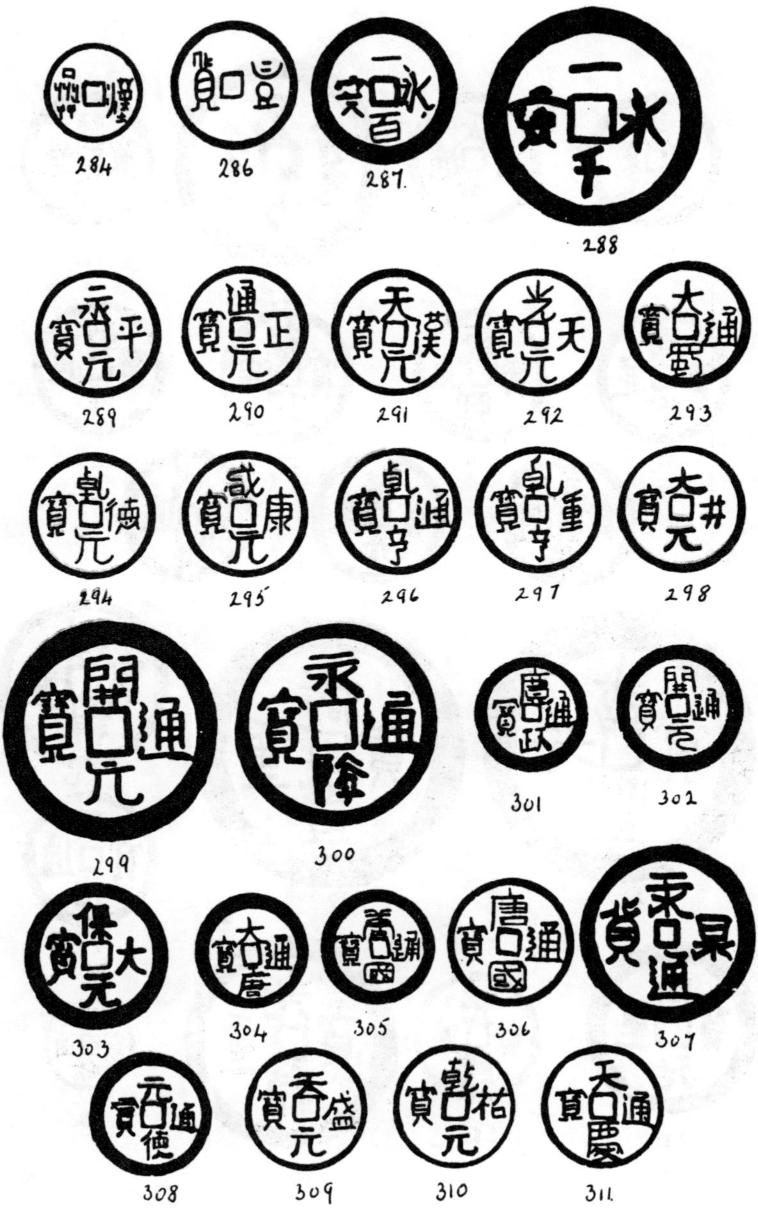

284 286 287. 288

289 290 291 292 293

294 295 296 297 298

299 300 301 302

303 304 305 306 307

308 309 310 311.

312.

313

314

315

316

317

319

320

321

322

323

324

325

326

327

328

329

330

331

332

333

334

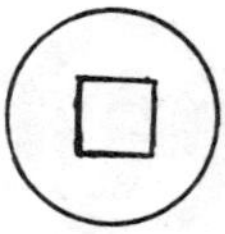

335

336

337

338

339

340

341

342

343

344

345

346

347

348

349

350

351

352

353

354

355

356

357

358

359

360

361

362

363

364

365

366

367

368

369

370

INDEX

(References to Obverse Types, not pages)

DYNASTIC TITLES

RULERS

LEGENDS

NOTES

NOTES